A View from the Perch

A View from the Perch

A collection of financial short stories, blogs, and other musings

William Robert Parrott

To Mi Abeulo

Acknowledgments

A huge thank you to my lovely wife, Tonya, and my amazing daughter, Hannah, for their endless love, laughter, and support.

A special thank you to my parents, Bill and Barbara Parrott, and my in-laws, Saundra and Duncan Murray, for their editing expertise, guidance, and advice.

Also by William R. Parrott:

Up the Income Ladder: Generate More Income in Retirement

*If history were taught in the form of stories,
it would never be forgotten.*
— Rudyard Kipling

Contents

	Contents	0
1	Once Upon a Time…	1
2	Buy Bonds or Bye Bonds?	2
3	Financial Planning Is a (Boston) Marathon and Not a Sprint	4
4	Do You Invest and Plan Like Captain Ahab or Captain Phillips?	6
5	Jacob's (Bond) Ladder	8
6	Let's Buy Two!	10
7	We Can't Win!	12
8	What Will the Stock Market Do Today?	14
9	Financial Planning Is Great Until…	16
10	Are You Using All Your Options to Generate Income?	18
11	My Fee Will Be Less than $2 Million	20
12	Planes, Trains, and Indices	22
13	Do You Remember March 24, 1980?	24
14	Matt Damon, The Martian, and You!	27
15	A Day in the Life of a Market Correction	30

16	There Will be Blood!	33
17	It's Time to Sell. Everything!	36
18	The Natural	39
19	Talk to Me, Goose	41
20	What If You Live to Age 101?	43
21	Can You Pick Stocks?	46
22	Have You Ever Been in a (Financial) Traffic Jam?	48
23	Retirement. Heads or Tails?	51
24	Peaks and Valleys	53
25	Do You Work with a Financial Cupbearer?	55
26	Roll Tide!	57
27	Can You Pick the Winner in the Crowd?	59
28	Are You a Home Run Hitter?	62
29	Did You Miss the Boat?	64
30	How's Your Bracket?	67
31	Where's the Beef?	69
32	145,830,932 of You Are Concerned about Retirement	71
33	Financial Pesticides	74

34	Are You Rich?	77
35	A Market Runs Through It	80
36	What Now Steph Curry?	83
37	Sell in May and Go Away?	86
38	Hey! Teacher!	88
39	The Stock Market Is Overvalued!	91
40	The Old Man and the Sea	93
41	Bend, Oregon	95
42	Are Forest Fires Good?	97
43	The Graduate	100
44	Rates Are Rising! Buy Bonds?	103
45	June Gloom	106
46	The Five Best Ways to Run Out of Money	108
47	Boardwalk, Marvin Gardens, or St. James Place?	111
48	Beware of Falling Interest Rates?	114
49	Fish and Chips	117
50	California, Texas, or Britain?	119
51	My Week at a Dude Ranch	122

52	There's Gold in Them Thar Hills!	124
53	Women and Poverty	126
54	Are We There Yet?	129
55	A Runner's Guide to Retirement Planning	131
56	Playing with Legos	135
57	BUY, BUY, BUY, SELL, SELL, SELL…	138
58	Market Top. Now What?	141
59	Money Follows the Heart	143
60	Marcia, Marcia, Marcia!	146
61	My, How Time Flies!	149
62	Five Rings. Five Things.	152
63	Happy Birthday National Park Service!	155
64	Dude, Where's My Car?	158
65	12 Reasons to Hire a Robo-Advisor	160
66	5 Lessons from Vin Scully	163
67	Ten Thousand Men of Harvard	166
68	"Mr. Speaker, The President of the United States!"	169
69	The Law of Large Numbers	172

70	Spooky Numbers	175
71	The Sun Will Come Up Tomorrow	178
72	Puzzle Pieces	181
73	Now What?	184
74	What's Up, Doc?	187
75	Do You Have Preferred Status?	190
76	Are You an Above-Average Driver?	193
77	15,902 Stock Picks for 2017	196
78	It Will Rain on May 23rd, 2025. At Noon	199
79	The Usual Suspects	202
80	Extra! Extra! Read All About It!	206
81	12c Things I Learned from My Calculator	208
82	Everybody Loves a Parade!	211
83	Sticks and Stones	214
84	Wax on. Wax off.	217
85	Are You a Control Freak?	220
86	Windsocks	223
87	Dump the Trump Bump?	226

88	The Watchman	229
89	Active vs. Passive vs. You	231
90	My Dog's Life	234
91	And the Oscar Goes To…	237
92	Balance	240
93	How to Survive a Stock Market Correction	243
94	Worse than a Stock Market Correction?	246
95	Shaw's Cove	249
96	By the People, For the People?	252
97	What's the YTB?	256
98	Should You Follow Your Dreams?	259
99	Spring Cleaning	263
100	Say What?	266
101	Time to Play It Safe?	268
102	Storage Wars	271
103	No Fear	273
104	Nothing but Net!	276
105	What's an Emerging Market Anyway?	278

106	Who Wants to Be a Millionaire?	281
107	Don't Read This If You're Under 50!	283
108	A Better Alternative?	286
109	A Letter to My Know-It-All Younger Self	289
110	What Will You Do in Retirement?	292
111	Are You Outperforming the Market?	297
112	Fishing from My Driveway	300
113	Worst Crash Ever?	302
114	Wonder Woman	306
115	Groundhog Day	310
116	First, Do No Harm	313
117	Are You an All-Star Investor?	316
118	Ready for a New Retirement?	320
119	Save It or Spend It?	324
120	Rock on Brother!	328
121	An Interview with Myself	331
122	10 Ways to Improve Your 401(k) Plan!	336
123	I'm Proud of You!	340

124	Will Stocks Rise Forever?	343
125	Can Stocks Go to Zero?	346
126	More, More, More!	350
127	How to Generate (More) Income in Retirement	353
128	My Friend Timms	357
129	The Bionic Advisor	359
130	New Beginnings	362
Notes and Disclaimers		**365**

1   Once Upon a Time…

When you hear those magical words, you know a story is coming. It may be a bedtime story you read to your children, or one told by a grandparent recalling a long-lost past. Stories have been passed down from generation to generation long before the written word. They've been used to educate, inform, and entertain people for centuries.

A View from The Perch is a collection of financial short stories, blogs, and other musings written to help you become a better investor. Each chapter is meant to stand on its own, so you can start on page 1 or 101. The date of each blog, along with the then-current level of the Dow Jones Industrial Average, is included to give you a better perspective of what was happening in the investment world at the time each one was written.

The stories address common investing themes like financial planning, asset allocation, diversification, fee awareness, and generational thinking. These financial pillars are repeated throughout the book and will give you guidance on how to improve your investment results.

I hope you enjoy the book.

So, let me tell you a story.

2   Buy Bonds or Bye Bonds?

When I entered the investment business in the late 80s, the yield on the 30-year U.S. Treasury Bond was above 8%. Investors were reluctant to buy them for fear of locking up their money for 30 years at 8% because they were convinced interest rates were going higher. A few investors remembered the double-digit yields from 1979 to 1984, and they were confident rates would again reach double digits. Twenty-five years later they're still waiting for rates to rise.

Today, with rates a fraction of where they were 25 years ago, investors are once again focused on rising rates. Investors are reluctant to buy bonds yielding 2% or 3% for fear of missing a rise in rates, so they keep their money in cash or a money market with a 0% yield. Even though rates are low, investors should not ignore the safety and income bonds can provide.

In the October 1, 2015 issue of *Fortune Magazine*, Josh Brown of Ritholz Wealth Management outlines a compelling case for owning bonds. He suggests that a portion of your portfolio be allocated to bonds to help "cushion a portfolio for down years."[1] He adds that stocks and bonds have only had three years where returns were both negative – 1931, 1941, and 1969. He recommends to readers to ladder their bond

---

[1] http://fortune.com/2015/09/30/next-bear-market/, Joshua M. Brown, September 30, 2015.

portfolio to help them with "a built-in defense mechanism against a gradually rising interest rate."[2]

I agree with Mr. Brown. Bonds should be added to portfolios to help protect investors against a falling stock market. A well-constructed bond ladder will also help investors with rising and falling interest rates.

In fact, bonds performed well during the market drops of 2002 and 2008. In 2002 when large cap stocks dropped 22.10%, long-term bonds rose 17.84%. In 2008 stocks fell 37% and bonds rose 25.87%.[3]

So, give bonds another look.

Bye, bye, and buy bonds.

Then you will go on your way in safety, and your foot will not stumble. ~ Proverbs 3:23

October 12, 2015

Dow Jones = 17,131.86

---

[2] See also Chapter 5, "Jacob's (Bond) Ladder."
[3] Dimensional Fund Advisors 2016 Matrix Book.

3   Financial Planning Is a (Boston) Marathon and Not a Sprint

In 2009, I decided to run the Boston Marathon. Because the Boston Marathon requires runners to qualify, the earliest I could run it would be in April 2011, so I launched my plan to make it happen and set out on a two-year journey to realize my dream.

In my early days of running marathons, I just ran without a plan. My first one was the Los Angeles Marathon in 1991. I was in shape but didn't have any type of strategy for race-day management. I was just going to run as fast as I could for as far as I could. I wore a cotton shirt and didn't stop at any aid stations to drink water. This "strategy" worked well until mile 20 when I started cramping because I was dehydrated. The last 6.2 miles were some of the worst of my life, and my lack of planning did me in.

Can this running analogy help you as an investor? I believe it can. I've noticed over my career that most investors don't have an investment strategy or financial plan. They show up on race day and hope for the best. This strategy usually doesn't end well. A well-constructed financial plan will assist you with income generation, portfolio construction, risk management, tax benefits, and estate protection.

A View from the Perch

In a paper titled "Financial Literacy and Planning: Implications for Retirement Wellbeing,"[1] Annamaria Lusardi and Olivia S. Mitchell revealed that successful planners – individuals with a financial plan – had three times the net worth of individuals who did little or no planning. This is significant and shouldn't be ignored. As Eleanor Roosevelt once said, "It takes as much energy to hope as it does to plan."

How did I do with my Boston Marathon plan? I qualified for the 2011 race, and it was perfect. The weather, the crowd, the course, and my time all exceeded my expectations. I set a personal record thanks to my two-year plan.

Do you not know that in a race all the runners run, but only one gets the prize? Run in such a way as to get the prize. ~ 1 Corinthians 9:24

October 19, 2015

Dow Jones = 17,230.54

---

[1] "Financial Literacy and Planning: Implications for Retirement Wellbeing," Annamaria Lusardi and Olivia S. Mitchell, NBER Working Paper No. 17078, Issued May 2011, http://www.nber.org/papers/w17078.

4 Do You Invest and Plan Like Captain Ahab or Captain Phillips?

Herman Melville's *Moby Dick* is full of colorful characters and packed with a ton of suspense. Captain Ahab obsessively pursues Moby Dick and wants revenge on the white whale. When I finished reading it, my first thought was Captain Ahab didn't have any plan to capture the whale. His only plan was to kill Moby Dick at any cost. In the end, the entire crew of the Pequod is killed because of Captain Ahab's thoughtless pursuit. If he had a plan, his results may have been different.

Maybe you saw the movie *Captain Phillips*, starring Tom Hanks, about the hijacking of the *Maersk Alabama*. He was the captain of the ship and a man with a plan. Captain Phillips ran numerous drills to make sure his crew was always prepared. He drilled them often so when trouble arrived he and his crew would be ready for action. He saved his ship, crew, and ultimately himself as the result of having a plan.

Do you identify with Captain Ahab or Captain Phillips when it comes to your financial planning and investment readiness? Do you hop in a boat and set sail chasing white whales or do you set a course to your financial destination? I'd say most investors are Captain Ahabs and don't have a plan. They're always chasing something – rumor, stock tip, return, or yield. If you plan and invest like Captain Phillips, your chances of success will increase. Investors with a plan are more likely to achieve their goals than those who don't. Nonetheless, once your plan is in place you'll need to review it often so you're ready for whatever the markets toss your way.

I encourage you to spend some time planning your financial future, so you can end up like Captain Phillips and not like Captain Ahab.

So God created the great creatures of the sea...~ Genesis 1:21

October 27, 2015

Dow Jones = 17,581.43

5   Jacob's (Bond) Ladder

Jacob's Ladder is an American horror movie starring Tim Robbins.

It's a horror story for investors when interest rates rise because when they rise, bond prices drop. The price of a bond is inversely related to interest rates, like a see-saw in a park when one side goes up the other side goes down. The price of a 30-year bond today would fall 17.6% with a 1% rise in interest rates. To add to this horror story the 30-year U.S. Treasury bond is currently yielding 2.85%. So, the thought of getting a single digit interest rate while losing 17% of your principal isn't too appealing.

How can you avoid this horror show? A bond ladder may protect you against rising and falling interest rates. It can be constructed with any type of bond or fixed income investment. You can create it with CDs, corporate bonds, tax-free municipal bonds, or U.S. Treasury investments. The choice is yours.

What's a bond ladder? It's a portfolio of bonds with different maturities. For example, a five-year ladder will own bonds maturing at one-year intervals: 1-year, 2-year, 3-year, 4-year, and 5-year. When the 1-year bond matures, you'll re-invest the proceeds into a new 5-year bond. The other bonds will each move up by one year, so your 2-year bond is now a 1-year bond and so on. By employing this strategy you'll always have money coming due, so you can take advantage of the current interest rate environment. This strategy can continue indefinitely.

What if interest rates fall? In this case your longer-term bonds will appreciate because when rates fall, bonds rise. A 1% drop in rates will make a 30-year bond appreciate by 22.8%! You'll have the ability take advantage of any type of interest rate move.

Bond ladders aren't scary, and they can help you avoid your own investment horror show.

Be strong and courageous. ~ Deuteronomy 31:6

October 29, 2015

Dow Jones = 17,755.80

6 Let's Buy Two!

Mr. Cub, Ernie Banks, was famous for saying, "Let's play two!" Mr. Banks was the long-time great shortstop for the Chicago Cubs and, as the story goes, Mr. Banks arrived at the ballpark in Chicago with the temperature hovering around 105 degrees and said, "Beautiful day, let's play two!"

Several years ago, I completed a financial plan for a couple. The exercise of compiling their data to make sure they were on track was very comforting to them. It gave them the confidence to know they were going to be fine financially. After the plan had been completed, the wife gave me a call to inquire about buying a new car. She wanted to make sure they had the resources to make the purchase. I told her she could buy two. I gave her my instantaneous answer because we had just finished their plan. I knew she and her husband had more than enough money to last a lifetime. The financial plan is not only beneficial to the client but also the planner. The financial plan puts the planner and the client on the same page. We were in sync with regard to financial information, so the decision for her to buy a new car was an easy one.

How many cars can you buy? Not sure? A solid financial plan can help you answer many of life's financial questions from buying a car to funding your retirement. The financial plan is your road map to your financial destination. The comfort in knowing where your assets are and what they are doing can be liberating.

A View from the Perch

As a note, she ended up buying one car – a Toyota Corolla.

"For I know the plans I have for you," declares the Lord, "plans to prosper you and not to harm you, plans to give you hope and a future." ~ Jeremiah 29:11

November 2, 2015

Dow Jones = 17,828.76

7   We Can't Win!

When my daughter was in the first-grade, I had the honor of coaching her soccer team, the Mustangs. These little Mustangs consisted of a band of young ladies, most of whom were playing an organized sport for the first time. Our league didn't keep score as the main goal was to introduce them to the world of soccer. Before our first game one of the girls on the team said to me, "If we don't keep score, we can't win." She was right.

Most investors don't keep score and they don't know if they are winning or losing the investment game. In addition, they don't know what game they're playing or what road they're travelling on. As the Cheshire Cat said to Alice in *Alice in Wonderland*, if you don't know where you are going, then it doesn't matter what road you take.

How can you win? How do you know if you're on the right road to achieving financial success? Here are a few ways to keep score:

Financial Plan. A well-designed financial plan will help you keep score and guide you towards your financial goals.

Investment Policy Statement (IPS). Your IPS will highlight how your investment holdings will be managed. In addition, it should also list your fee schedule and how often your account will be reviewed.

Quarterly Reviews. The quarterly review is a check-in to review the activity in the previous quarter and to see if any changes need to be made to your plan.

Annual Review. The annual review is a deeper dive into your financial plan and investment policy statement. When should you schedule your annual review? I'd recommend scheduling these meetings around your birthday.

As a note, the girls kept score at each game.

The person that said winning isn't everything, never won anything. ~ Mia Hamm

November 9, 2015

Dow Jones = 17,730.48

8   What Will the Stock Market Do Today?

Paul called me every Monday morning to ask what the stock market was going to do for the week. He wanted to know if he should make any changes to his account because of what might happen. Of course, I had no idea what it was going to do during the day or the week. Paul was well read and asked great questions about stocks, the stock market, and the economy. He kept me on my toes. The interesting thing about Paul's weekly call was that he didn't own one share of stock – not a single share! Paul's portfolio consisted entirely of bonds. He owned an assortment of CDs, U.S. Treasuries, and corporate bonds. When he'd ask me if the stock market going down would hurt his account, I told him it could go to zero and he'd be fine. In fact, if the stock market was going down, his bonds would perform well.

Investors have a daily fascination with the stock market. It's hard to ignore CNBC and other financial television shows covering every tick as if it were a sporting event.

How does the stock market compare to some of the titans in the sporting industry? On an annual basis, the market has "won" 73% of the time![1] John Wooden, legendary basketball coach for the UCLA Bruins, had a winning percentage of 80%. Bill Belichick, the current head coach of the New England Patriots, has a winning percentage of 71%. Scotty Bowman,

---

[1] Ibbotson®SBBI® 2015 Classic Yearbook.

former head coach of the Detroit Red Wings, won 63% of his games. Joe Torre, former manager of the New York Yankees, won 54% of his games. I'd say the stock market is in pretty good company.

On a rolling 20-year period, of which there have been 70 since 1926, the stock market is undefeated. It's made money 100% of the time![2]

So, don't worry about what the stock market is doing today because it's a waste of your time and energy: instead, focus on your financial plan and your long-term goals.

"I have told you these things, so that in me you may have peace. In this world you will have trouble. But take heart! I have overcome the world." ~ John 16:33

November 16, 2015

Dow Jones = 17,483.01

---

[2] Ibid.

9   Financial Planning Is Great Until...

Financial Planning is great until life gets in the way and then you got to do what you got to do. I'm a big fan of financial planning. It's what I do for a living. A financial plan can help individuals organize their financial lives and guide them to a path of independence.

However, I'm aware of the pitfalls of financial planning. It does take time for clients to compile and gather their data. The interview requires the client to bare their financial soul, a challenge since most people don't like to talk about money.

What's a family to do when life gets in the way of their plan? I'd recommend focusing on four areas: cash, debt, retirement, and education.

First, take an inventory of your assets. Once completed, increase your cash level so you have enough money set aside for a rainy day. It will help reduce your dependence on debt. A suggested amount is three to six months of your household expenses. If your family expenses are $5,000 per month, then your cash goal should be $15,000 to $30,000.

Next, review your retirement accounts. You want to make sure you're contributing to your company retirement plan. You can contribute up to $18,000 to your 401(k) each year. If you're 50 or older, you can contribute an extra $6,000 for a total of

$24,000. You can also make an IRA contribution of $5,500 or $6,500 if you're over 50.

Third, comes debt. "Debt" is a four-letter word, and it should be eliminated as soon as possible. A high-interest, non-deductible debt such as a credit card or auto loan should be paid off first. How much debt is too much? Your debt limit should be no more than 38% of your total household gross income. If your income is $10,000 per month, your total monthly debt payments should be $3,800 or less.

Funding your children's education accounts comes last. Your offspring can apply for a loan or scholarship for college, but you won't be able to get a scholarship for retirement.

Finally, start today to take care of your financial affairs. If you know where the leaks are, you'll be able to plug them up over time.

Let our advance worrying become advance thinking and planning. ~ Winston Churchill

November 30, 2015

Dow Jones = 17,719.92

10   Are You Using All Your Options to Generate Income?

Investors are constantly searching for extra ways to generate income. Traditional income investments like CDs and U.S. Treasuries, corporate, and municipal bonds are yielding historically low interest rates. What's an income investor to do?

The option market may be your answer for generating more income. If you own individual stocks or Exchange Traded Funds (ETFs), you can turn these holdings into income producing machines. The most conservative option strategy is to sell a call or write an option on a stock you currently own.

Let's look at a hypothetical example of using an option on a fictitious company. In our example, you own 1,000 shares of ABC Company purchased for $21 a share. A few years later it' selling for $43 and you want to sell it at $45. You could wait until it traded to $45 to sell your shares. You could also enter a limit order to sell your shares at $45. The third way is to use the option market to sell your ABC shares at $45. Here's how it works. One option contract controls 100 shares of stock.

If you own 1,000 shares of ABC, you'll sell ten option contracts (1,000/100 = 10). Option contracts expire on a weekly basis, so you can match your selling time horizon to any week of the year. The strike price is the price where you want to sell your stock, in this case $45 per share. The income you receive is called the option premium.

A View from the Perch

Let's pick the December 18, 2015 ABC $45 strike price. The contract generates $1 in premium for the ABC $45 strike price or $1,000 in income (before fees) to your account. The money will be credited to your account at the time of the trade and is yours to keep regardless of what happens to the price of ABC stock. If it closes at $45 or higher on December 18th, you're obligated to sell your stock. If it closes at $44.99 or lower, you keep your shares. If you retain your shares in ABC, you can repeat this process next month.

Options involve risk and aren't suitable for every investor. It's important to work with a firm or an advisor who fully understands your investment goals and the characteristics of options.

Ask and it will be given to you; seek and you will find; knock and the door will be opened to you. ~ Matthew 7:7

December 7, 2015

Dow Jones = 17,730.51

11   My Fee Will Be Less than $2 Million

In the mid-90s I received a call from a client asking me how I invest a lot of money. I asked him how much money. He was reluctant to give me an answer at first because of the large sum. He eventually had to tell me the amount, so I could give him my advice. He had received an inheritance from the estate of his uncle. He was both delighted and nervous about receiving this substantial sum. When the money arrived, we decided to invest it in a 6-month U.S. Treasury Bill to give us time to develop a plan while taking advantage of the government guarantee.

His uncle didn't have an estate plan. As a result, my client had to write a check to the IRS for more than $2 million to cover his uncle's estate tax. This was a tough pill to swallow. He had just written the largest check of his life and it went to pay taxes!

Next, we started to build a game plan so his beneficiaries wouldn't be burdened with sending one red cent to the government when he and his wife passed away. I referred him to an attorney who helped him establish several trusts to protect his assets for generations to come. I assembled a portfolio of California tax-free municipal bonds and high-quality dividend-paying stocks.

What's behind the $2 million fee? Not long after he wrote his check to the IRS, he asked me what the fee would be to set up the investment accounts and family trusts. I told him the fee will be less than $2 million. He got a nice chuckle from my comment.

He and his wife passed away a few years ago and the trusts and investments are still going strong today and, more importantly, his beneficiaries didn't send any money to the IRS for estate taxes.

A little planning can go a long way for you and your family!

Take delight in the Lord, and he will give you the desires of your heart. ~ Psalm 37:4

December 14, 2015

Dow Jones = 17,368.50

12   Planes, Trains, and Indices

Planes, Trains and Automobiles is a great movie starring Steve Martin and John Candy. Steve Martin and John Candy use all necessary means to get home for the holidays, and Steve Martin doesn't care how he gets there. As we launch another investing year, should you be more concerned with outperforming an index or arriving at your financial destination? It's common for investors to focus on an index, usually the Standard & Poor's 500, as their primary benchmark. An investor will consider their year successful if they outperformed the index even if it was down for the year. Relative outperformance is considered a victory for most.

Standard & Poor's website tracks over 700,000 indices in real time. 700,000! If you were going to benchmark to an index, which one of the 700,000 indices would you choose? If you're an investor with a diversified portfolio, you may only have 15% or 20% exposure to companies in the S&P 500. Most of your portfolio will be linked to some other asset class like small companies, international companies, bonds, real estate, commodities, or cash. These asset classes will have little, if any, correlation to the S&P 500 index. I recommend that you broaden your market benchmark to combine all your asset classes. A blended benchmark will give you a better picture of your overall portfolio performance.

If I'm scheduled to fly from Los Angeles to New York should I be concerned with other planes flying to Bend, Austin, or Denver? Should I be concerned there is more than one flight to New York and some of the planes will arrive before mine does? No! My only concern is to arrive in New York on my scheduled flight.

As you travel through 2016, focus on your own goals and don't worry about which one of the 700,000 indices is up, down, or sideways. Your portfolio and financial plan should be firmly tied to your hopes and dreams and no one else's. If you arrive at your financial destination on your terms, this should be considered a huge success!

The journey not the arrival matters. ~ T.S. Eliot

January 4, 2016

Dow Jones = 17,148.94

13   Do You Remember March 24, 1980?

Do you remember March 24, 1980? I don't. I was 15. I was probably concerned with three things. Was I going to the beach? Were the Dodgers going to win? Where were my friends and I going to eat lunch? I probably went to the beach, the Dodgers undoubtedly won, and I most likely went to McDonald's.

On March 24, 1980, the S&P 500 dropped more than 3%. I'm sure the morning headlines were full of doom and gloom. The "experts" were almost certainly publicizing this as the beginning of the end, and the buy and hold strategy was over forever.

If you were fortunate enough to buy the S&P 500 Index on that horrible day and held it until the end of 2015, you made a lot of money. Let's say you purchased $10,000 worth of the Vanguard S&P 500 Index Fund on March 24, 1980. Your investment today would be worth $506,785, giving you an average annual return of 11.59%.[1]

What if you had the foresight to buy McDonald's stock after eating your Big Mac on that frightful down day? If you gobbled up $10,000 worth of McDonald's stock, your original investment would now be worth $2.19 million, giving you an average annual return of 16.25%! During this run in McDonald's stock, you would have received $307,052 in

---

[1] Morningstar Office Hypothetical Tool.
[2] Ibid.

dividends. In 2015 your dividends from your original $10,000 investment were $38,363![2]

I believe the buy and hold strategy is the best one to pursue for most investors. When the market drops, it gives you an opportunity to invest in great companies at lower prices. It's like flying. The only way to get on an airplane is when it's on the ground. If you're not on the plane when the pilot leaves the gate and roars down the runway, you're not getting on.

It's difficult to buy during a market meltdown, so here are a few suggestions to help strengthen your portfolio:

- If you need your money in one year or less, don't invest in the stock market. Keep your money in cash or short-term CDs.
- If you're going to retire in five years or less, keep three years' worth of expenses in cash, short term CDs or U.S. Treasuries.
- If you're concerned about international turmoil, invest in small and mid-cap companies headquartered in the U.S. They typically don't have any international exposure.
- Add dividend-paying companies to your portfolio. According to Morningstar, there are

over 1,000 companies that currently yield more than 3%.[3]
- Asset allocation and diversification still work. A balanced portfolio of stocks, bonds and cash will treat you well over the long term.
- If your investment time horizon is three to five years or more, you should hold on to your investments.

Current market conditions aren't fun, but this can be an opportunity to reexamine your investment holdings and financial goals to make sure they're still in line with your long term financial plan.

Be on your guard, stand firm in the faith; be courageous; be strong. ~ 1 Corinthians 16:13

January 7, 2016

Dow Jones = *16,514.10*

---

[3] Morningstar Office.

14   Matt Damon, The Martian, and You!

Mark Watney, played by Matt Damon, is stranded on Mars after a violent storm in *The Martian*. He's forced to use several tactics to survive and regain contact with his crew back on Earth.

Let's imagine you accompany Mr. Watney to Mars. Your Mars mission will leave Earth on January 1, 1990. Before you leave, you contact your investment advisor to give her instructions on how to invest your life savings. You tell her to buy three mutual funds and hold them until you return. This trip will be quick, so you're not worried about investing in these funds. She will invest $100,000 into each of the following funds: The Vanguard S&P 500 Index Fund, The Vanguard Small Cap Index Fund and the American Funds EuroPacific Mutual Fund. Your $300,000 portfolio is diversified across large, small, and international companies. After the meeting, you write down the prices of the S&P 500 and Dow Jones Industrial Average on a 3 x 5 card and put it in your pocket. The indices on December 31, 1989 were, respectively, 353.40 and 2,753.20.

Once you arrive on Mars, you're caught in a violent storm and realize you'll be there for a long time. You now have no way to communicate with your advisor to check your investments.

After 26 years on Mars, you return to Earth and the first thing you do is read the headlines from the newspapers and realize it's been nothing but doom and gloom. The frightful headlines have you more worried than ever. You're convinced your $300,000 nest egg has been wiped out. You remember your 3 x 5 card in your pocket. You pull it out to compare it to the current value of the markets. You're shocked! How can the S&P 500 be at 1,192.03 and the DJIA at 16,346.45? It doesn't make any sense. During your time on Mars the S&P 500 went up 443% and the DJIA rose 493%. Amazing.

You now frantically search for your investment account statements. As you rip open your statements you're floored at the results. How can this be? It isn't possible! Tears of joy begin to flow. Your $300,000 investment is now worth $3.17 million![1] Your investment has increased over 10 times! During your 26 years on Mars, they had an average annual return of 9.49%!

After further review, you notice that five times during this 26-year run your accounts had a one-year gain of 30% or more. The best year was 2003, when your investments rose 35.70%. The worst year occurred in 2008, when your assets fell 37.94%. From 2000 to 2002 your account had three consecutive down years. It ended a calendar year with a negative return seven times, but it made money 73% of the time.

We're now in the middle of a storm and the urge to sell stocks is high. At times like this it's important to stop and take inventory of your holdings. You can't go to Mars to get away from all the noise, but you can go to a small island in the

---

[1] Morningstar Office Hypothetical Tool.

Caribbean or South Pacific for a few years and let your investments run.

He replied, "You of little faith, why are you so afraid?" ~ Matthew 8:26

January 11, 2016

Dow Jones = 16,398.57

15   A Day in the Life of a Market Correction

The global stock markets continue to swoon. Each morning I wake up and check to see what the stock market has in store for the day. I look at my phone (AAPL, T) to view the latest news. I turn on my TV (SNE, TWX) to CNBC (CMCSA). While I watch CNBC (CMCSA) I scan my email accounts (GOOG, MSFT). Once I run through the news, I then pick over Facebook (FB), LinkedIn (LNKD), and Twitter (TWTR) to get caught up on the latest social media.

After my morning channel checks are done, I grab breakfast and eat some Honey Nut Cheerios (GIS) with a glass of Tropicana Orange Juice (PEP). While eating my breakfast I listen to ESPN Radio (DIS) on satellite radio (SIRI).

After breakfast, I go for a run (NKE, UA) to get in a little exercise. I ran my little loop in 19:31 – not a bad time.

It is now time to get ready for work, so I take a shower, shave (PG), and get dressed (JWN). On the way to work, I stop at the local gas station to fill up (XOM, AXP) my truck (TM). I was happy it only cost me $19.87! With a full tank of gas, I drive to Starbuck's (SBUX, AXP) to get coffee which cost me $5.08.

After my trip to Starbucks (SBUX, AXP), I make a brief visit to my bank (WFC) to get an extra $20.00 for the day. I take a detour to Target (TGT, AXP) to get a few office supplies. The office supplies cost me $20.02

A View from the Perch

At the office, I turn on my computer (HPQ, MSFT) to start my work day. I use Yahoo Finance! (YHOO), Morningstar (MORN), and Value Line (VALU) to keep abreast of the market.

At lunch, I head to McDonald's (MCD, AXP) to get a burger, fries, and a Coke (KO).

Back at the office, I decide to order a book from Amazon (AMZN, AXP), which is shipped to my house via UPS (UPS). The book cost me $20.08.

The market had another rough day, so I went home and took my dog (WOOF) for a walk.

After my walk, my wife and I went to dinner at Eddie V's (DRI) to get something to eat and have a glass of wine (STZ).

I'm now back at home to catch up on the day in sports (DIS, TWX) and check the latest social media feeds (FB, LNKD, TWTR, GOOG, MSFT). Until tomorrow…

What if you invested $10,000 in each of these companies when they became publicly traded? Your "everyday" portfolio would consist of 34 companies and cost $340,000. Your first purchase was in 1972, your last in 2015. This "everyday" portfolio generated an average annual return of 14.67% from June 1, 1972 to December 31, 2015.[1] Your $340,000 investment is now worth $38,624,889 and you received $4,524,932 in dividend income.[2]

---

[1] Morningstar Office Hypothetical Tool.
[2] Ibid.

Your everyday portfolio is almost as good as winning the lottery. Down days are no fun but remember they do occur and eventually stocks recover. Life goes on so stay invested and enjoy the long-term, upward trend of the stock market.

The real key to making money in stocks is not to get scared out of them. ~ Peter Lynch

January 15, 2016

Dow Jones = 15,988.08

16   There Will be Blood!

There Will be Blood is a 2007 movie starring Daniel Day-Lewis. The movie is based on Upton Sinclair's book *Oil!* His book was published in 1927 and dealt with the struggles of greed and fear many faced in the early days of the oil industry in Southern California. I'm sure if Mr. Sinclair were writing his book today, 89 years later, the story line would be similar.

The price of oil has been identified as one of the main culprits for this stock market drop. Below is a comparison of some of the major drops in the price of oil since 1948.[1] As you can see, this decline in oil is like previous oil corrections:

- May 1980 to April 1986 the price dropped 77.24%.
- October 1990 to December 1998 the price dropped 74.43%.
- July 2008 to February 2009 the price dropped 69.59%.
- November 2000 to January 2002 the price dropped 43.78%.
- April 2011 through January 2016, the recent low, the price of oil is down 69.59%.

---

[1] http://www.macrotrends.net/1369/crude-oil-price-history-chart.

It's interesting to review the price of oil from May 1980 to December 1998, when it declined 85.75%. The Standard & Poor's 500 stock market index during this same timeframe climbed 1,005%, considered by some to be the greatest bull market in history. This 18-year bull market in stocks averaged 17.59% per year. During this bull run there were 2,526 up days and 2,193 down days. One of the down days during this bull run included October 19, 1987, when the stock market dropped 25.73%.

I'm not calling a bottom in oil. However, if the phone rang I'd answer it.

What should you do today? Stay diversified and focus on your financial goals.

As stocks continue to fall, bonds are performing well. Income generated from stocks, bonds, and funds will continue to pay you regardless of the price of the underlying asset so stay invested.

As a reminder, the stock market has always recovered. It might be one week, one month, or one year, but it has always bounced back. If you need proof, please look at the following years: 1907, 1915, 1929, 1930, 1931, 1932, 1934, 1937, 1939, 1940, 1941, 1946, 1953, 1957, 1962, 1966, 1969, 1973, 1974, 1977, 1981, 1990, 2000, 2001, 2002, and 2008.

Therefore, do not worry about tomorrow, for tomorrow will worry about itself. Each day has enough trouble of its own. ~ Matthew 6:34.

A View from the Perch

January 25, 2016

Dow Jones = 15,885.22

17   It's Time to Sell. Everything!

Is it time to sell everything? You shouldn't sell everything, but you may want to sell something. The stock market continues to underwhelm, and this trend looks like it may remain in the near term. The fear of the downside is real and growing among investors, especially if you pay attention to posts, papers, and pundits. The consensus among the masses is for the doom and gloom to linger.

Should you be a seller? Here is a list of individuals who should sell their stock holdings.

Sell if you need your money in one year or less. According to Morningstar and Ibbotson the stock market has made money 73% of the time on a one-year basis between the years of 1926 and 2014. However, this range is wide. The best year was 1933, with a gain of 53.99%, and the worst was 1931, with a loss of 43.34%.[1]

Sell if you're going to buy something with the money invested in the stock market. If you're going to buy a home, car, boat, or plane, then this money should be invested in cash.

Sell if you must pay for an event like a wedding or a college education. My daughter will be leaving the nest soon for college. As a result, I sold half of her investment account two

---

[1] Ibbotson® SBBI® 2015 Classic Yearbook.

years ago and invested the proceeds in U.S. Treasuries, knowing her tuition payment is imminent.

Sell if you're retiring in three to five years. You don't need to sell all your stock holdings – just enough to cover three years' worth of household expenses.

Sell if you're up to your eyeballs in debt. This can be mortgage, credit card, consumer, student, auto, or margin debt. Debt is debt, and the less you have of it the better. Your total monthly debt payments should be less than 38% of your gross income.

Sell if you don't have a financial plan. If you don't, it's like driving a car without a steering wheel or sailing a ship without a rudder. How can you invest your assets if you have no idea where you're going? A financial plan will help guide your investments and make you a better investor.

Sell if your account is 100% invested in stocks. A portfolio invested in 100% stocks has had an average annual return of 10.1% with a standard deviation of 20.1. A portfolio with 70% stocks and 30% bonds has had an annual return of 9.2% and a standard deviation of 14.3. The bonds reduced your risk by 29% and your returns by 0.9% per year.[2]

Sell your holdings if you can find a superior long-term investment to outperform great American and international companies.

---

[2] Ibid.

If you don't fall into one of the above categories, you should be a buyer of stocks!

Happy Investing.

The Lord has done it this very day; let us rejoice today and be glad. ~ Psalm 118:24

January 29, 2016

Dow Jones = 16,466.30

18   The Natural

The Natural is one of the best baseball books of all time. It was written in 1952 by Bernard Malamud and later adapted into a movie starring Robert Redford.

Roy Hobbs is a young man with a gift for throwing fastballs for strikes. He was 19 when he was shot in a Chicago hotel room before his baseball career started. Roy had to wait 16 years before returning to the game, when he joined the New York Knights as an outfielder and single handedly saved them from financial ruin with his beloved "Wonder Boy" baseball bat. Roy Hobbs was forced to be patient before he was to become the best there ever was. Mr. Hobbs' overnight success was 16 years in the making.

What does Roy Hobbs have to do with investing? Investing requires patience and focus, both of which served Mr. Hobbs well. These two traits, more than any other, are the key ingredients for long term investment success.

It'd be nice if stocks rose swiftly and substantially. However, this isn't the case. It may take years for a stock to realize its full potential. As a matter of fact, legendary investor Peter Lynch said in his book, *One Up on Wall Street*, that he may hold a stock for three to five years before the investment realizes a substantial profit. I've often said a stock only goes down twice: the first time is right after you buy it and the second is when you need the money the most.

Facebook is a classic example of a stock that needed patience. It went public in 2012 and quickly lost a third of its value before it started to rise to dramatic heights.

How about Apple? An investor who purchased $10,000 worth of Apple stock in 1980 and held it to the beginning of 1998 saw their value increase by $8 to $10,008.

What about Big Blue? Investors who purchased IBM stock in 1962 had to wait until 1997 before they doubled their money.

Do you want fries with your order? An investor who bought McDonalds stock in 1972 had to wait until 1982 before the burger chain started to show some real bite. If you added Coke to your happy meal, you had to wait until 1986 before you realized a profit from this bellwether.

A Boeing investor in 1972 had to wait four years before it took off.

I know it's hard to be patient in this Twitter, Snapchat, Instagram world but you need it to turn small assets into big assets.

But if we hope for what we do not yet have, we wait for it patiently. ~ Romans 8:25

February 8, 2016

Dow Jones = 16,027.05

19 Talk to Me, Goose

Thirty years is a long time. Thirty years ago, the year 1986, brought us *Top Gun*, the Chicago Bears, and the Challenger Space Shuttle tragedy. The yield on the United States Treasury 30-year bond is currently 2.61%. It's hard to imagine investing in this bond today and waiting until 2046 for it to mature. However, there are individuals buying it for safety because of the recent stock market turmoil. Safety is a relative term, of course. A bond is certainly "safer" than a stock in the short term, but over the long haul, it's hard to beat a basket of stocks.

According to Morningstar, there are currently 3,892 companies with a dividend yield more than 2.61%.[1] Included in this list are 264 companies that have raised their dividend at an average annual rate of 10% or more during the past 10 years.

I plucked 10 companies from the list of 264: Boeing, Harley-Davidson, Intel, McDonald's, Microsoft, Pepsi, Walmart, Paychex, Aflac, and Target. An investor who purchased these companies and invested $10,000 in each would've spent $100,000. They are now worth $9.29 million, generating an average annual return of 19.47%.[2] The current dividend income from this portfolio is $245,846 which is 145% more than your original investment.

---

[1] Morningstar Office.
[2] Morningstar Office Hypothetical Tool.

Today, this portfolio yields 3.18% and generates $3,180 in income from a $100,000 portfolio while the U.S. Treasury 30-year bond generates $2,610. This basket of stocks will give you $570 more in income plus upside.

I'll take my chances with a basket of stocks with a strong history of paying and raising dividends. A diversified portfolio of companies with solid balance sheets and dependable cash flows is tough to beat.

For wisdom is more precious than rubies, and nothing you desire can compare with her. ~ Proverbs 8:11

February 12, 2016

Dow Jones = 15,973.84

20   What If You Live to Age 101?

Are you financially prepared to live to age 101? It would be terrible to live to the ripe age of 101 only to run out of money at age 91. This risk of outliving your money is called longevity risk, and it's a real concern. It's especially a concern for those individuals who sell their stock holdings due to short-term fluctuations in the stock market. It may seem prudent to sell your stocks when they're going down and wait for them to recover before you buy them again. However, when will you know the stock market has bottomed and started to recover? When the stock market is off to a rough start to the year, the urge to sell may be high. Is this a wise move? I believe it's a horrible move and could cost you dearly, especially if you live to 101.

According to the 2010 U.S. Census there were 53,364 individuals aged 100. In 1980 there were 32,194 centenarians. A low estimate of 240,000 centenarians is expected by the year 2046. Will you be part of this elite crowd? If you're female, your chances of reaching this magical age is much higher than it is for men. The U.S. Census Bureau says 82.8% of the centenarians are women.

A 50-year-old person today with annual household expenses of $100,000 will see this number rise to $451,542 due to inflation by the time they reach age 101! If you sold your stocks today and moved your money into a savings account to wait for the stock market storm to pass you'd have to wait a long time to double your money. How long? If you placed your cash in a Wells Fargo Platinum Savings Account earning 0.01%, it would take you 6,943 years to double your money!

Another risk in parking your money in a savings account is inflation. With your money in a savings account, you might not be losing it in the stock market but you're losing it to inflation. $100,000 in a cash account today will be worth $22,146 (inflation adjusted) in 51 years. Your purchasing power drops 78% by the year 2067.

How can you keep pace with inflation? You need to own stocks of all shapes and sizes – large, small, and international. You need to own stocks in good times and bad. A portfolio of stocks will give you the best opportunity to beat inflation especially over the long haul.

Investors who bought the Vanguard S&P 500 Index Fund in March of 1999, during the "best" of times, would have averaged 4.2% on their investment through the end of January 2016. This same investor who bought this fund in March of 2009 at the "worst" of times would have averaged 16.94%.[1] Of course, it's unlikely you'll buy at the top or bottom, so continue to add to your account on a regular basis.

I'd recommend ignoring the noise urging you to sell your stocks at the wrong time. Instead, focus on your financial plan and long-term investment goals.

---

[1] Morningstar Office Hypothetical Tool.

Even now the one who reaps draws a wage and harvests a crop for eternal life, so that the sower and the reaper may be glad together. ~ John 4:36

February 15, 2016

Dow Jones = 16,196.41

21   Can You Pick Stocks?

By now you've probably have heard of the FANG stocks. The FANG consists of Facebook, Amazon, Netflix, and Google. These four stocks had quite the run in 2015, returning 82.72% to those who were fortunate enough to buy them on January 1, 2015 and hold them through December 31, 2015. Were you part of this elite crowd?

How about a pinch of SALT? The SALT group is Stamps.com, Autobytel, Loton Corp., and Tri-State 1st Banc. SALT returned 83.01% for calendar year 2015. If you had owned some SALT, you'd have outperformed FANG by a pinch.

Say WHAT? What if you purchased WHAT? This cohort returned 160.07% in 2015. The WHAT group consisted of Wayfair Inc., Heron Therapeutics, Anacor Pharmaceuticals, and Tile Shop Holdings. Did you own some WHAT?

How about DOME? The Domers blew the roof off the FANGs. DOME returned 199.57% last year. The DOME lineup included Dycom Industries, Omega Protein Corporation, Meritage Hospitality Group, and Eagle Pharmaceuticals.

What if you bought the wrong FANG? If you bought Fresh Market, Anadarko Petroleum, NuStar GP Holdings, and Geospace Technology you would have lost 40.96%. This FANG would have taken a big bite out of your financial assets.[1]

---

[1] Source: Morningstar Office Hypothetical Tool.

It's unlikely you owned any or all these combinations last year. Does this make you a great stock picker or a bad stock picker? I'd say neither. Is there a better way to capture stellar stock market returns?

Most investors would be better served with spending their free time working on their financial plan. It will help you determine your asset allocation and investment selection. Once it's completed, I'd recommend buying a basket of low-cost mutual funds diversified around the globe. This strategy is less stressful than trying to find the next FANG!

One of the funny things about the stock market is that every time one person buys, another sells, and both think they are astute. ~ William Feather

February 19, 2016

Dow Jones = 16,391.99

22 Have You Ever Been in a (Financial) Traffic Jam?

Have you ever been in a traffic jam? If you've driven on the 5, 10, 15, 405, 101, 110, 40, 70, 35, 91, or 95 it's likely you've been stuck in one. At any point during the traffic jam did you ever contemplate getting out of your car and walking, thinking it would get you to your destination faster?

The drive from Austin to Dallas on I-35 takes about 3 ½ hours. On I-35 there are more than enough opportunities to get stuck in a traffic jam. However, I've never contemplated walking to Dallas from Austin because of these minor traffic jams. According to Google Maps it would take me 64 hours or about two and a half days to walk this route. I don't like traffic jams but they're part of driving.

In the early 1970s my mom, sister, and I went to visit my cousins in Laguna Beach. We spent the day at the beach and stayed for dinner. On the way home to Los Angeles we were caught in the mother of all traffic jams and I didn't handle it well because it was dark, and we weren't moving. I was convinced the end of the world was near and I'd never see my dad, my other sister, or my friends again. My fears were unfounded because at some point the traffic started flowing again, and we made it home without incident.

What does a traffic jam have to do with investing? In tough times when the stock market is not cooperating, investors want to bail out and sell their investment holdings and wait for the market to give them the all-clear signal.

Let's look at three different mutual funds you could've purchased from January of 2001 to January of 2016.

The Investment Company of America mutual fund had a 15-year return of 5.22% while the individual investor in this same fund generated 3.91%. A $100,000 investment in this fund would have returned $214,523 if you stayed the course. The investor return was $177,770. The investor left $36,752 on the table.[1]

The Vanguard S&P 500 mutual fund, the patriarch of all funds, had a 15-year return of 4.28% while the investor made a 2.03% return. $100,000 in this fund would have grown to $187,506. The investor made $135,181, losing out on $52,324.[2]

Fidelity Magellan fund had a 15-year return of 2.72% while the investor in this fund lost 1.19%. $100,000 in the Magellan fund is now worth $149,563. The investor's $100,000 is now worth $83,562, a difference of $66,001.[3]

An investor who invested in these three funds and stayed the course would have picked up an extra $155,077 for their account.

---

[1] Morningstar Office Hypothetical Tool: January 1, 2001–January 31, 2016.
[2] Ibid.
[3] Ibid.

It doesn't pay to buy and sell because of headlines or market conditions. The next time you run into a financial traffic jam, remember it will eventually pass.

Drivers today can access several tools to help them get to their destination safely. With GPS it's easy to navigate the nation's highways. Like a GPS for your car, a financial plan can be your GPS and pilot you through today's markets, allowing you to focus on your long-term investment goals.

There are no traffic jams along the extra mile. ~ Roger Staubach

February 22, 2016

Dow Jones = 16,620.66

23   Retirement. Heads or Tails?

There are two sides to a coin – heads and tails. Like a coin, retirement has two sides – financial and emotional. The financial side of retirement is easier, because you either have enough money to retire or you don't.

The other side of retirement is emotional, and it can't be calculated on a spreadsheet. It's like jumping over a three-foot crevasse that's 100 miles deep. You know this short leap isn't an issue, but part of your brain is questioning your wisdom in making the attempt. What if, by chance, you don't make it to the other side and crash into the abyss?

On the emotional side of retirement, you and your family need to answer several questions with little to do with numbers. For example, what will you do with your life once you stop working? Will you continue to live in your current home or city? Will you move to the beach, the mountains, or a big ranch in the middle of nowhere? Will you move to where your children and grandchildren live? Will you live with your children? How about hobbies? Can you fish, golf, hike, bike, or surf every day? Will you be a volunteer at the local school or join a non-profit? These are just of few of the questions you should ask yourself before you retire.

After working for 40 or 50 years, it's not easy to flip a switch and do nothing. Will you be able to transition into retirement at 100% or do you need to ease into your life of luxury? Once retired you'll need new routines and activities to keep you engaged and active. Will your new schedule coincide with your spouse's? Your spouse might not want you in the house 24/7.

I once worked with an individual who went through the financial planning process to see if he could financially afford to retire. His financial numbers were solid, and he could retire on his terms. After I ran the first financial plan, I ran another, then another, then another, then another and so on. I believe we generated eight or nine plans before he was ready to retire. We explored every financial scenario, and with each passing plan the numbers barely budged. Financially, he'd be fine. His hurdle to retirement was emotional. I don't think he was ready to make the leap into retirement and may have hoped his plan would've forced him to work a few more years. I'm happy to say after our last plan he was emotionally ready to retire.

I've worked with many retirees over the years who were able to make the three-foot leap over the 100-mile crevasse. The retirees who successfully made it to the other side all wish they'd have retired sooner. Are you ready to make the leap?

Come to me, all you who are weary and burdened, and I will give you rest. ~ Matthew 11:28

February 25, 2016

Dow Jones = 16,697.29

24 Peaks and Valleys

Last summer, my wife and I hiked to the top of Estes Cone, located inside the Rocky Mountain National Park. We started in a valley at the trailhead to Long's Peak and marched along the Eugenia Mine Trail towards the summit of Estes Cone at an elevation of 11,006 feet. It wasn't a fourteener, but it was still taxing.

For most of our hike, we were in a valley surrounded by gigantic trees and massive rocks and were unable to see the top of Estes Cone. I had faith we were on the right path because we had a trail map, a compass, our friends, and a guide. I knew if we stayed on the trail we were going to reach the summit. Hikers who get into trouble don't pay attention to their map or they decide to leave the trail. Once atop Estes Cone, we were treated to an amazing 360-degree view. We could see Long's Peak, Twin Sisters, the town of Estes Park, and much more. Our time on the summit, however, was short lived because a lightning storm was fast approaching.

When the stock market is in the valley it's easy to lose sight of your goal. It's where investors are most likely to make poor investment decisions and abandon their financial plans. It might appear safe and wise to seek the shelter of a savings account or money market fund and wait for the storm to pass. But this mistake could leave a long-term dent in your portfolio. The Dow Jones Industrial Average dropped over 11% to start this year. Since February 11th, it has climbed 7.5%. The market is still not back to the peak of the year, but it looks a lot better today than it did a few weeks ago. Any investors who left the trail during the market trough and abandoned their plans missed out on a nice little rebound.

If you stay on the trail and follow your plan, you'll arrive at your destination. It's the time you spend in the valley that will allow you to enjoy the view from the summit. As a matter of fact, you can't reach the summit unless you go through the valley.

Even though I walk through the darkest valley, I will fear no evil, for you are with me; your rod and your staff, they comfort me. ~ Psalm 23:4

February 28, 2016

Dow Jones = 16,516.50

25 Do You Work with a Financial Cupbearer?

The cupbearer was a confidant of the king and held in high esteem. He was the person tasked to taste the king's wine to make sure it was poison free. If the cupbearer drank the wine and lived, it was safe for the king to drink generously. Obviously, if the cupbearer died after drinking the wine, the king would get a new glass of wine and a new cupbearer. The cupbearer was hired to protect the king and he had to put his interest below the king's.

The Department of Labor is currently deciding the fate of the fiduciary standard for the investment industry. Who's a fiduciary? What's advice? Should your interests come first? The questions go on and on.

Registered investment advisors already adhere to the fiduciary standard, meaning they operate under the Investment Advisers Act of 1940.[1] An investment professional who's not a registered investment advisor only has to make a suitable recommendation to the client. It would seem obvious for advisors to put their clients' interests first, but some

---

[1] "Choosing A Financial Advisor: Suitability vs. Fiduciary Standards," Ryan C. Fuhrmann, CFA, November 17, 2011, https://www.investopedia.com/articles/professionaleducation/11/suitability-fiduciary-standards.asp.

advisors have not done so, and therefore the Department of Labor is involved. In my opinion, every investment professional should act as a fiduciary, regardless of title, and always put their clients' interest first.

I'd suggest taking the fiduciary standard one step further. I believe advisors should act as a financial cupbearer for their clients and show clients their personal investment holdings. This full disclosure suggestion is like a presidential candidate releasing his/her tax returns. How does your advisor invest his life savings? Does he own stocks, bonds, or funds? Is he buying or selling? A quick peak at your advisor's holdings will tell you a lot about their investment philosophy.

Do you work with a financial cupbearer?

…For I was the king's cupbearer. ~ Nehemiah 1:11

March 3, 2016

Dow Jones = 16,943.90

26   Roll Tide!

I've observed a few things during my lifetime that I know to be true. The sun rises in the east and sets in the west. The tide comes in and it goes out. The spring always follows the winter. The stock market rises, and it falls. As Kevin Bacon said in *A Few Good Men*, "These are the facts of the case, and they are undisputed." So, it's amazing to me when the stock market goes down and investors run for the hills and sell their equity holdings.

According to *The Financial Times*, investors pulled $60 billion out of mutual funds in January.[1] Do you know what happened in February and the first few days of March? An investor who cashed out on January 20th of this year would've missed a 10% rebound in the S&P 500 index. Instead, individuals who sold during the dark days of the market probably locked in a little loss. In this same article, Lipper reports that the last time this much money flowed out of mutual funds was in September of 2008. If you bought stocks during the 2008 meltdown you would've enjoyed an annual return of 8.91% through February 2016. A $10,000 investment into the Vanguard S&P 500 fund on September 15, 2008 is now worth $18,898![2]

Successful long-term investors don't panic when others do. One suggestion is to type into your phone or write on a 3 x 5

---

[1] Investors pull more than $60bn from mutual funds in January, Attracta Mooney and Chris Newlands, 2/28/16.
[2] Morningstar Office Hypothetical Tool.

card: "The market is down, what can I buy?" A contrarian investor will buy when others are selling, allowing them to purchase stocks at a more favorable price. When you see a sea of red in the stock market, the time to buy may be near. It's challenging to be a buyer when the "experts" in the media are hollering the end of the world is near, but this is one of the best times to spend some money on high-quality companies.

Two roads diverged in a wood, and I – I took the one less traveled by, and that has made all the difference. ~ Robert Frost

March 7, 2016

Dow Jones = 17,073.95

27   Can You Pick the Winner in the Crowd?

The Los Angeles, Chicago, New York, Boston, Berlin, and London marathons attract thousands of runners each year. The runners have different abilities and backgrounds, but they all have the same goal: finishing the race. How would you pick a winner for an upcoming marathon? Would you ask a friend? Maybe get your advice from a TV commentator? Throw a dart? Subscribe to a service specializing in picking the best marathon runners? How about looking at the field to identify the one who looked like the best runner? Can you review past race results to isolate the winner? It's not easy predicting the winner.

In reality, only five or six runners in the field of thousands will have a legitimate chance of winning. Does this make your job of picking the winner easier? The elite runners will leave the field behind after the first mile and the pack will never see them again. They'll finish the marathon in just over two hours. The field will average about four hours with the back of the pack finishing in six, seven, or eight hours. And some runners won't finish.

According to the Morningstar database, there are 21,015 stocks. Is it possible to pick the best five or six stocks every year from the tens of thousands? Can you pick the five best? Five worst? What if your stock didn't finish the race? In 2015, there were 1,074 companies that were up more than 95% and 626 companies that were down more than 95%.[1]

What's the best way to stay in the race so you finish your financial marathon? I recommend taking the field. The average time from last year's Boston Marathon was 3:46. Ask any marathon runner if she'd like to finish a marathon in 3:46. She'd probably say, "yes."

The ideal way to take the field when you invest is to own an index fund. The Vanguard S&P 500 Index fund has averaged 10.64% from August 1976 to February 2016. A $100,000 investment is now worth $5.44 million![2] I'd bet most investors would be happy with these results. Of course, to increase your odds of winning the investment race, you'll want to own a diversified basket of funds.

As a runner in a marathon, you're competing against professional athletes, finely tuned runners, weekend warriors, and first-time runners. A runner dedicated to training for a marathon will have an enjoyable experience. An individual with little training, not so much.

Like a marathon runner, an individual who enters the investing arena will be competing against professionals, seasoned traders, hobbyists, and first-time investors. If you're not ready for the competition, it would be wise to hire a financial advisor to help you reach your goals.

---

[1] Morningstar Office.
[2] Morningstar Office Hypothetical Tool.

Is it worth your time to try to find the best five companies every year? A better allocation of your time is to identify your top financial goals, with the help of a Certified Financial Planner, and make your dreams become reality.

Running is the greatest metaphor for life, because you get out of it what you put into it. ~ Oprah Winfrey

March 10, 2016

Dow Jones = 16,995.13

28   Are You a Home Run Hitter?

There are few events in sports more exciting than a home run. Kirk Gibson's spectacular home run to beat the Oakland A's in game 1 of the 1988 World Series is my favorite. Carlton Fisk's colorful home run in the 1975 World Series against the Cincinnati Reds was incredible. Aaron Boone's game 7 home run against the Boston Red Sox, sending the Yankees to the 2003 World Series, is as about as dramatic as you can get.

Do you need to hit a homerun every time you buy a stock to reach your financial goals? Is it necessary to swing for the fence each time you purchase a stock? It'd be nice to hit a four bagger with every stock purchase, but it's not crucial for you to achieve financial success.

Tony Gwynn was one of my favorite baseball players. He was a legendary hitter who played his entire career for the San Diego Padres. He finished his amazing career with a .338 batting average and 3,141 hits, earning him a spot in Major League Baseball's Hall of Fame. He wasn't known for hitting home runs. During his fabled 20-year career, he only hit 135 home runs. By comparison, Hank Aaron hammered 755, and Babe Ruth swatted 714. Tony Gwynn made a career of hitting singles and doubles.

How can you employ an investment strategy of hitting singles and doubles? A time-tested strategy is to buy dividend paying companies with a history of growing their dividend. A company who pays a consistent and growing dividend is the equivalent of hitting singles and doubles. According to the website Dividend.com, companies who increased their dividends generated an average annual return of 10.07% from January 31, 1972 to December 31, 2013 while non-dividend paying companies averaged just 2.34% during this same timeframe. In fact, dividend paying companies outperformed non-dividend paying companies in both up and down markets, with less risk.

While waiting for your next stock home run you can happily feast on a steady stream of dividend income.

…being strengthened with all power according to his glorious might so that you may have great endurance and patience… ~ Colossians 1:11

March 16, 2016

Dow Jones = 17,325.76

29   Did You Miss the Boat?

The stock market is now positive for 2016, to the dismay of many. Did you miss the boat? Did you abandon ship in January? Is it too late to get back into the market? The Dow Jones Industrial Average is now up 14% from the January 20 low and has climbed over 2,100 points over the last eight weeks. The rebound has been fast and furious.

In January, investors sold billions of dollars' worth of stock and decided to seek refuge on the dock while waiting for the storm to pass. A few brave souls left the safety of the dock and decided to buy during the depth of the storm. The riders of the storm were rewarded for their bravery.

What do you do if your ship left you on the dock because you were too timid to venture out into the raging storm? Should you chase the market and start buying again? Here are a few suggestions for those of you who were left behind.

- During the aftermath of any storm it's a good idea to reassess your situation. What are your financial goals? What's your time horizon? If you have more than three years before you need your money, you should continue to purchase stocks.
- What is your current allocation? Did missing the rebound in the market leave a gaping hole in

your equity allocation? If so, you should buy stocks to balance your accounts.
- Are there sectors in the stock market that may help you achieve your long-term goals? Is it time to add healthcare, energy, or financials to your portfolio? How about small or international companies? If you're missing a few sectors, it's time to increase your equity exposure.
- You can wait patiently for the next storm to arrive. As any sea captain knows there's always another storm on the horizon. When the next one arrives, you can take advantage of the displacement of prices to acquire solid companies at lower prices.
- It may be time to rebalance your portfolio. When you rebalance, it brings your account back to its original asset allocation.
- Is it time to chart your financial plan? A financial plan will be your radar to help guide you through the nastiest of financial storms.
- The buy and hold model still works, so sometimes the best strategy is to batten down the hatches and hold on for a wild ride. When the sun rises in the morning, you'll be glad you stayed the course.

Investing through a storm is never easy. In a raging storm or a calm sea, it's best to navigate the financial waters with a financial plan. It will assist you in times of distress and keep you from abandoning ship.

He that will not sail till all dangers are over must never put to sea. ~ Thomas Fuller

March 19, 2016

Dow Jones = 17,623.87

30   How's Your Bracket?

Kansas? Michigan State? Austin Peay? Is your final-four bracket still intact? According to ESPN, only 1,140 of the 13 million entrants (.009%) picked the correct final four. A concentrated bet on your alma mater to win the tournament may still bear fruit if you attended Oklahoma, UNC, Villanova, or Syracuse. If you went to any other school, you'll have to wait until next year.

On January 13th, Westgate SuperBook had Syracuse as a 1,000 to 1 bet to win the entire tournament. A nice pay-off if the Orange should win it all. Michigan State was originally listed as a favorite with odds of 5 to 1 to win the tournament. You lost 100% of a bet you placed it on Sparty. If you pick 8 or 16 teams to win the tournament, your odds of having a team in the final game rise dramatically. A diversified basket of teams may keep you in the running to win your bracket.

How can the bracket help your investing?

A concentrated bet on one stock may or may not work out. If you're concentrated in the right investment, your portfolio will perform well. A portfolio of Apple, Berkshire Hathaway, or McDonald's has treated investors well over the years. However, if you owned Enron or WorldCom, your entire investment would have been wiped out.

A stock controlling more than 25% of your portfolio is a concentrated bet. What should you do if you're holding a concentrated position? If possible, reduce it to 5% or 10% of your investment portfolio. With the extra money, you can add additional investments to diversify your portfolio.

A diversified portfolio of index funds can keep you in the investment game. Investing across sectors, categories and borders will do well over time.

Investing should be more like watching paint dry or watching grass grow. If you want excitement, take $800 and go to Las Vegas. ~ Paul Samuelson

March 28, 2016

Dow Jones = 17,535.39

31   Where's the Beef?

Where's the beef? You may remember the successful ad campaign from Wendy's. The little old lady in the commercial was looking for the beef between two massive hamburger buns. Investors today may have the same feeling when they look at interest rates. Where's the rate?

Interest rates continue to drop. The yield on the U.S. Ten Year Treasury is 1.77%, a drop of 21% for 2016. Individuals looking for income ideas continue to be frustrated by the lack of opportunities. One method for countering this trend is to turn an equity investment into an income producing asset.

How can you take advantage of the long-term trend in the stock market to generate income from your investments? A systematic withdrawal plan can turn your equity holdings into income-producing assets. This strategy allows you to sell a fixed dollar or percentage from your mutual fund holding. The amount sold from the funds can be paid to you monthly.

As an example, let's say you invest $100,000 in XYZ mutual fund. After you invest, you decide to withdraw 5% of the account balance on an annual basis. This, initially, will generate $5,000 per year or $416 per month. If your fund grows 8% per year and you're removing 5%, your investment is growing at 3%.

Let's look at a real-world example. The Vanguard Standard & Poor 500 Index Fund (VFINX) has been around since August 31, 1976. Let's say you invested $100,000 in 1976 and decided to withdraw 5% of your account balance each year. After 39 years, you received $843,697 in distributions and the value of your account is now worth $746,734. Your first-year distribution in 1976 was $5,120 and in 2015 it was $36,254,[1] an increase of 608%! The systematic withdrawal plan is a total return strategy using all the resources of your mutual fund holding.

For this strategy to work you must be a buy and hold investor. If you invested in this fund from 1976 you endured Black Monday, the Tech Wreck, and the Great Recession. However, after the drops, this fund managed to generate an average annual return of 12.05%.[2]

If you are looking for income-generating ideas, look beyond traditional bond investments and focus on your equity holdings.

It is better to have a permanent income than to be fascinating. ~ Oscar Wilde

March 31, 2016

Dow Jones = 17,685.09

---

[1] Morningstar Office Hypothetical Tool.
[2] Ibid.

32 145,830,932 of You Are Concerned about Retirement

Fifty-nine percent of individuals over the age of 18 are concerned they won't have enough money for retirement, according to an April 2014 Gallup Poll. Are you one of the 145,830,932 individuals? How do you know if you'll have enough money for retirement? What should you do if you're in this group? What can be done today to improve your financial foundation?

Here are some strategies for those of you who are concerned about not having enough money.

First, complete a financial plan. Your plan will help define your financial life, including your retirement. The planning process will help you focus your thoughts on what's important for you and your family. It will identify the strengths and weakness of your current financial situation and give you suggestions on how to save for a successful retirement.

It's paramount to save as much as you can towards your retirement. Every bit of savings you can muster will improve your financial situation. If you're currently saving $500 per month, can you bump it to $600? Saving $500 per month earning 5% will grow to $205,516 in 20 years. An increase to $600 will give you $246,620, or $41,104 more.

What if you're not able to save more? In this situation, review your investment allocation and tilt your account towards stocks. Over time, an aggressive profile will outperform a conservative one. A more aggressive account may cause you heartache in the short-term but will benefit you in the long run.

Besides saving more, try spending less. I get a kick out of commercials telling you: "The more you buy, the more you save." Instead of buying five tubs of peanut butter, buy six and "save" 10% on your total order. However, the best way to save is not to spend.

Creating a budget is essential. Reviewing your spending habits will identify the good, bad, and ugly of your spending. It will put you in a better position to see where your money is going. Reviewing your bank and credit card statements from the past four to six months will give you a picture of where and how you've spent your money. After your review, is there a category or two you can reduce or eliminate? If so, you can transfer these extra dollars into your monthly savings program.

The last strategy is working longer. Really? Who wants to work longer? I don't. If you don't want to work longer, then I'd focus on saving more and spending less.

Twenty years from now you will be more disappointed by the things you didn't do than by the ones you did do. So throw off the bowlines. Sail away from the safe harbor. Catch the trade winds in your sails. Explore. Dream. Discover. ~ Mark Twain

A View from the Perch

April 4, 2016

Dow Jones = 17,737.00

33   Financial Pesticides

Pesticides kill. They're created to kill weeds, insects, and rodents. These toxins are spread by everything from small spray bottles to crop dusters.

In the late 1980s, swarms of helicopters would fly over Los Angeles spraying pesticides trying to kill the fruit fly. They'd fly low and dispense poison on everything – homes, pets, people, and the fruit fly. As the fleet of helicopters flew over my house I remember thinking this can't be good. Thankfully, it only lasted a few months.

Financial pesticides also kill, and they can destroy your long-term investment performance. Here are a few:

High fees. The higher your fee, the lower your return. Have you reviewed the fee structure for your investments? I was reviewing a client's investment held at another firm and the fee for her fund was over 2.5%. She wasn't aware her fee was so high because she never received an invoice or noticed it on her statement. I told her she would never see the fee as it was priced into her fund holding. She wasn't happy and decided to move her money to a more economically desirable investment.

Excessive trading. The more you trade, the more fees you'll pay. In addition to increased trading costs, you may trigger short-term capital gains, taxed as ordinary income. Excessive trading and short-term capital gains can be damaging to your long-term returns.

Actively traded mutual funds. According to Morningstar, most active fund managers fail to beat their benchmark.[1] The "stock-pickers" failed to deliver returns above their corresponding index. Active funds also have higher fees than index funds.

Timing the market. Trying to time the market is futile. To do it correctly you must pick the right stock at the right time – consistently. It can't be done. Market timing will add to your trading costs and expose you to short-term capital gain taxes. You may also miss opportunities if your timing is off.

Being impatient. Your investments may take two, three, or more years before they show a substantial gain. Impatient investors usually buy and sell at the wrong time. A redwood tree will grow to over 300 feet, but it won't do it in a day.

Fear. Fear of losing money will keep investors out of the market – especially during a market drop. Billions of dollars left the stock market in January in search of safety. When the market turned around, it left these investors on the sideline.

No plan. Investing and trading without a financial plan is toxic. A plan will help guide your investing and improve your long-term results. Your plan should include an investment policy statement outlining your asset allocation strategy, fee structure, and investment selection.

---

[1] https://corporate.morningstar.com/us/documents/MarketCommentary/MMC_2016_Q1.pdf.

How can you avoid financial pesticides? Be patient. Have a plan. Purchase low-cost investments. Stay diversified. Review your accounts often. If you follow these guidelines, good things can happen.

Whoever is patient has great understanding, but one who is quick-tempered displays folly. ~ Proverbs 14:29

April 11, 2016

Dow Jones = 17,556.41

34   Are You Rich?

Are you rich? How do you know? It depends, of course, where you live. In Malawi, the per capita income is $255. In Somalia, $542; Haiti, $824; United States, $54,629; Luxembourg, $116,612.[1]

According to the Pew Research Center, 71% of the world's population, about 5 billion people, live on less than $10 per day.[2] What can you buy for $10? A few of the top selling items on Amazon costing $10 or less are Super Glue, Uno, Frisbee, and a jumbo muffin pan. If you lived on $10 per day would you buy a jumbo muffin pan?

Can your wealth help the 71% living on less? I believe so.

How much money should you give away? A tithe, or 10%, is suggested. Malachi 3:10 sums it up pretty well: *"Bring the whole tithe into the storehouse, that there may be food in my house. Test me in this," says the Lord Almighty, "and see if I will not throw open the floodgates of heaven and pour out so much blessing that there will not be room enough to store it."*

How to give? Here are a few ideas:

---

[1] Per Capita data is from the World Bank (2014).
[2] http://www.pewresearch.org/fact-tank/2015/09/23/seven-in-ten-people-globally-live-on-10-or-less-per-day/, Rakesh Kochhar, February 23, 2015.

Create a philanthropic plan. A giving strategy should be incorporated with your financial plan. It will focus your charitable efforts on causes you support.

Give monthly. Why wait until December?

Dividends and interest. A portfolio of stocks and bonds will generate an income stream for giving. You can give the income and keep your principal.

Appreciated assets. An asset with an unrealized gain is a good candidate for a donation. It will benefit the organization and you. They get the asset; you get a deduction while avoiding a capital gains tax.

Systematic withdrawal plan. Selling a fixed percentage or dollar amount each month from a mutual fund is a good way to donate money to others. It will allow you to budget your giving.

Cash. Cash is earning nothing, so you might as well turn it into an asset to help others.

I must warn you, once you start giving you won't be able to stop. The ROI on your philanthropic activity can't be calculated on a spreadsheet, but give anyway.

The best definition of wealth I heard was from a fraternity brother of mine. He said, "I'm a rich man. I'm not rich monetarily but rich with friends, family, and faith."

Are you rich?

A View from the Perch

You might not make it to the top, but if you are doing what you love, there is much more happiness there than being rich or famous. ~ Tony Hawk

April 15, 2016

Dow Jones = 17,897.46

35   A Market Runs Through It

Fly fishing is addictive. It's more a religion than a sport for many. Its attraction, in addition to catching fish, is the gear: rod, reel, line, leaders, waders, snips, and flies.

A River Runs Through It isn't a fly-fishing movie per se, but it does show amazing scenes on the Blackfoot River. If the fly-fishing scenes in the movie don't get you excited about fishing, nothing will.

The river I fish is nothing like the Blackfoot. It's slow and meandering. The water is dark and murky, and I have no idea where the fish are hanging out. I cast a lot, and I'm forced to be patient. I cast. I wait. I cast. I wait. On occasion I will pull a nice little fish out of the water.

What does fly fishing have in common with investing? Plenty.

My time on the water begins the evening before, when I build my plan. Where to fish? What rod to use? What's the best fly? It doesn't matter if you're fishing or investing: a thoughtful plan will increase your chance of success. It will make both fishing and investing more enjoyable.

Investing, like fishing, requires persistence. Persistence brings patience. Patience gives you discipline. Discipline will make you a better investor. It would be nice to catch a 20-pound bass with each cast, but I know it's not going to happen. On most casts I come up with air and water. It's important to keep casting because the only way to catch a fish is if the fly is in the water. A disciplined investor will stay invested to catch the long-term trend of the stock market.

The fly is half the fun in fly fishing. Choosing the right fly is part of the challenge. What fly to use – popper, dragon fly, minnow, crawfish? I've used them all at one point or another. A diversified box of flies is a must because conditions change quickly. Markets change quickly as well. A diversified portfolio of stocks, bonds and cash will keep you ready for most market conditions.

A wind knot is not fun because a tangled line is downtime. When I'm confronted with a wind knot, I have two choices. I can untangle the knot or cut the line. I've done both. During my downtime, I review my goals. Should I keep fishing? Am I in the right spot? Do I need to add a heavier line? When the market corrects, and your portfolio is in a knot, what do you do? You can't ignore a wind knot when fishing – it must be dealt with. A market correction is the same. Don't ignore it. Use a correction to review your holdings and goals.

Hiking to the lake or river can be just as fun as fishing. Investors seem to be in a hurry to arrive at their destination. Take time on your journey to enjoy the view. Investing is a lifetime event. It doesn't start with your first job nor does it end with your last. Investing is generational.

Planning, persistence, and long-term thinking are needed for fly fishing and investing. If you practice these things, you'll be hooked for life.

***If fishing is a religion, fly fishing is the high church.* ~ Tom Brokaw**

April 19, 2016

Dow Jones = 18,053.60

36   What Now Steph Curry?

One of the splash brothers is down! It's heartbreaking to think Steph Curry might miss the rest of the playoffs after his incredible, record-setting season. The Warriors were destined to win another NBA title before Mr. Curry was injured.

The Warriors aren't alone in losing a superstar. The LA Clippers lost two – Chris Paul and Blake Griffin. The odds for the Warriors and Clippers to win the NBA title dropped after the injuries. Their loss, however, is San Antonio's gain. The Spurs' chances of winning the title are now almost even with the Warriors.[1]

The Warriors lost 20% of their starting five while the Clippers lost 40%.

How would your investment portfolio perform if 20% or 40% of it were "injured"? What if you bet on a "star" stock and it got hurt? Apple has been a longtime fan favorite, but recently it has fallen on hard times. It's down 26% from its all-time high, causing a lot of pain for investors. All is not lost, however. If you had invested $100,000 in Apple 10 years ago, it's now worth $1.3 million, generating an average annual return of 29.34%.[2] Apple, like Curry, will once again return to glory.

---

[1] www.oddssharkcom/nba/nba-futures; website accessed April 27, 2016.
[2] Morningstar Office Hypothetical Tool.

What to do if you have a chunk of your assets in one or two high-flying stocks? If you own a holding of 25% or more, this is considered a concentrated holding. Here are a few strategies you can employ to protect your investments:

Sell 10% or 15% of your holding to reduce its dominance over the rest of your account. Of course, you want to pay attention to capital gains if it's in a taxable account.

Purchase put options to protect your position. A put option will appreciate if your "star" holding falls in value. The gain in the put option may offset the loss in value from the drop in your stock. Buying puts on a regular basis will be expensive, especially if your stock continues to appreciate.

A zero-cost option collar can help offset the cost of buying puts. By selling a call option to generate income you'll be able to offset the cost to purchase your put option. The advantage to this strategy is that your out-of-pocket cost will be negligible to zero. The disadvantage is your gain in the stock will be capped by the selling of the call option.

A diversified portfolio will lower your dependence on a star player. As I mentioned, the Warrior's pain is the Spurs' gain. While Apple hasn't performed well, other investments have. Amazon, McDonald's, Time Warner, Facebook, Alphabet, Home Depot, Altria, Lockheed Martin, Philip Morris, and Mondelez are all up 20% or more for the past 12 months.

A concentrated position is fun to own when it's appreciating in value but not so much when it starts to decline. It pays to pay attention to your position limits and asset allocation. Rebalancing your accounts once or twice a year will also help keep your holdings in check.

Then Jesus said to them, "Give back to Caesar what is Caesar's and to God what is God's." ~ Mark 12:17

April 27, 2016

Dow Jones = 18,041.55

37   Sell in May and Go Away?

Sell in May and go away? Catchy tune. Should you pay attention to this Wall Street axiom? Does it make sense to take six months off every year from your investment strategy?

A 35-year history of the Vanguard S&P 500 Index fund shows some interesting results. An investment on May 1, 1981 generated an average annual return of 10.84%. The returns jumped to 11.20% per year by waiting until November 1, 1981 to purchase this fund, a spread of .36%.[1]

Let's say your portfolio is worth $1,000,000 and it generates 2%, or $20,000, per year in income. If you sell in May and buy in November, you're giving up six months of income. You're leaving $10,000 on the table or 1% of your account value. What if you have $300,000 in unrealized gains? When you sell your fund, the gains become realized and you must pay a capital gains tax. A capital gains tax rate of 20% applied to your $300,000 gain will trigger a tax of $60,000. Thanks to the loss of income and your capital gains tax you have "lost" 7% of your account value.

Between 1950 and 2015 the month of May has returned .13% to investors. June has lost .10%. July gained .84%. August lost .27%. September lost .68%. October gained .80%.[2] A $1 million

---

[1] Morningstar Office Hypothetical Tool.
[2] http://www.moneychimp.com/features/monthly_returns.htm.

investment on May 1, with these average monthly returns, would be worth $1,007,130 at the end of October.

The buy and hold strategy for May to November generated a gain of $7,130. In addition, you received $10,000 in income for a total return of $17,130. This compares favorably to losing $70,000 because of something that "May" happen.

Let your stocks run. If the market drops, use it as an opportunity to buy quality companies to get ready for the November launch.

OCTOBER: This is one of the peculiarly dangerous months to speculate in stocks in. The other are July, January, September, April, November, May, March, June, December, August, and February. ~ Mark Twain

May 1, 2016

Dow Jones = 17,891.16

38   Hey! Teacher!

The cost of attending college keeps rising. The tuition inflation rate is about 6% per year.[1] What's the current annual cost of college? At a private university, expect to pay $42,224 while a public college will set you back $21,447.[2]

What are your options for sending little Johnny or Suzy to college?

Save and invest. The best way to pay for college is to save for it. When your child is born, start saving early and often. If you have a child today, you know in about 18 years they may attend college. You can identify a college and figure out how much it will cost to attend. With these two data points you can calculate how much money you need to save. When my daughter was born, I set up an investment account for her and started buying as much stock as I could afford. If you invested $100 monthly in the Dimensional Large Cap Value Fund (DFLVX) and Dimensional Small Cap Value Fund for 18 years you ended up with $111,600.[3] With $111,600 you can pay for a large portion of the tuition.

Scholarships. Can you rely on a scholarship? The number of students who receive a scholarship is low. The percentage of

---

[1] https://us.axa.com/goals/saving-for-college/questions/college-inflation-rate.html.
[2] https://bigfuture.collegeboard.org/find-colleges.
[3] Morningstar Office Hypothetical Tool.

students who receive a full ride is .3%, or 3 students per 1,000. An athlete will fare a little better at 2% or 20 students per 1,000.[4]

Student loans. In 2014 students borrowed $100 billion to finance college.[5] According to the latest figures the default rate for these loans is 10.7%. The lowest default rates were from students who attended four-rear private institutions (5.9%) and four-year public institutions (7.4%).[6] These are big numbers in both borrowing and defaults.

Junior college. It may pay to spend two years at a junior college before transferring to a four-year university. This path will help reduce your cost of attending a four-year college and increase the odds of transferring to the school of your choice.

No college. The percentage of kids who attend college after graduation is 65%.[7] What does this mean for the other 35% who don't go on to college? It's not good. The cost of not going to college is a lot more expensive than paying for college. According to the Pew Research Center, the unemployment rate for high school graduates is 12.2% and the percentage of

---

[4] https://www.cbsnews.com/news/how-rare-are-full-ride-scholarships/, Lynn O'Shaughnessy, Moneywatch, January 24, 2011.
[5] http://www.edcentral.org/edcyclopedia/federal-student-loan-default-rates/.
[6] Ibid.

[7] https://www.nytimes.com/2014/04/26/business/fewer-us-high-school-graduates-opt-for-college.html, Floyd Norris, April 25, 2014.

these former students living in poverty is 21.8%.[8] Dark numbers. The no-college option is not an option and should be avoided at all costs.

My recommendation is to budget and save for college. A budget will help you identify opportunities to cut costs and save money.

When I was in college, I wanted to be involved in things that would change the world. ~ Elon Musk

May 4, 2016

Dow Jones = 17,651.26

---

[8] http://www.pewsocialtrends.org/2014/02/11/the-rising-cost-of-not-going-to-college/.

39   The Stock Market Is Overvalued!

In 1990, I joined Dean Witter Reynolds, Inc. One of my early encounters was with a veteran broker who told me the stock market was overvalued and the price of silver was going to take off. His office was impressive with charts and graphs adorning his walls. He referred to the charts on the walls and gave me an education as to why silver was going to rise, and stocks were going to fall.

How did his prediction turn out?

In the first quarter of 1990 the price of silver was about $5.50 an ounce and it's currently trading at $17.52 an ounce.[1] Had I taken his advice and bought silver I would have averaged an annual return of 4.55% from 1990 to 2016. A $10,000 investment in silver is now worth $31,854.

How about stocks? The Dow Jones Industrial Average in January of 1990 was 2,590. Today it's 17,701, a gain of 583%, or 7.67% per year, without dividends.

Instead of silver, let's look at a few investments we could've purchased.

The Vanguard S&P 500 Index Fund during this stretch generated an average annual return of 9.11%. A $10,000 investment is now worth $99,556.[2]

---

[1] http://silverprice.org/silver-price-history.html.
[2] Morningstar Office Hypothetical – January 1990–April 2016.

A basket of Coke, Pepsi, and McDonald's returned 11.77% per year. A $10,000 investment is now worth $187,506.[3]

An investment in Apple, Microsoft, and Intel turned $10,000 into $854,264 for an average annual return of 18.39%.[4]

The 30-Year U.S. Treasury Bond was yielding 8.5% in 1990. Instead of buying silver an investor could've purchased a guaranteed investment paying 8.5% maturing in 2020. Who wouldn't want 8.5% guaranteed today?

This broker was persuasive and a good salesman. His case for buying silver and selling stocks was convincing, but I'm glad I didn't follow his advice.

For the past 25 years I've heard the stock market is overvalued and silver, gold, wheat, oil, etc. was going to outperform stocks. In the short-term this may be true, but I'll always place my bet on stocks for the long haul.

How much better to get wisdom than gold, to get insight rather than silver! ~ Proverbs 16:16

May 9, 2016

Dow Jones = 17,705.91

---

[3] Ibid.
[4] Ibid.

40   The Old Man and the Sea

The Old Man and the Sea is one of Hemingway's best novels. Santiago, the main character, is an aging fisherman. It had been over 80 days since he was able to catch a fish, so he decided to try his luck far from the shores of Cuba. He ventured out on his own and was rewarded with the catch of a lifetime by hooking a humongous marlin. It took him more than two days to bring it close enough for the kill. The fish was too big to fit in the boat, so he tied it to the side and headed back to shore. On the journey home several sharks attacked his marlin. He was successful in fending off a few sharks but by the time he returned home the marlin had been eaten to the bone.

Santiago was patient and goal oriented. Even though he was in a fishing slump he had a plan to catch his big fish by fishing alone far from the shores of his normal spot. He had to revise his old plan and take more risk to reach his goal.

What can you learn from Santiago?

Patience. When buying stocks, it pays to be patient. It's possible the stock you just purchased won't advance for some time. It could be days, months, or years before your stocks shows promise. It's important to give them time to flourish.

Goals. It's of paramount importance to have investment goals – especially when buying stocks. Do you want to retire early? Buy a new home? Travel the world? Help others? If you write your dreams down, they're more likely to come true.

Plan. Santiago had a plan and so should you. Your plan will guide you to where you need to be to reach your goals. A plan is the starting point for your future financial success.

Risk. You can't catch fish on land. Santiago had to take more risk to catch his fish. You may need to take more risk as well. It will be challenging to grow your wealth if you hold most of your assets in cash, CDs, or short-term bonds. You need stocks for the long-term growth of your wealth.

Perseverance. It took Santiago two days to land the marlin. He didn't give up on his goal amidst the struggle. At times the stock market doesn't cooperate, and you'll need fortitude to stay the course. Your stocks will go down and be attacked by haters and naysayers, but you must hold on – especially if you have conviction in your investment strategy.

Goals, planning and perseverance will help you be a successful investor. When your stocks are in a holding pattern think about Santiago and his battle with the mighty marlin.

For he and all his companions were astonished at the catch of fish they had taken. ~ Luke 5:9

May 12, 2016

Dow Jones = 17,720.50

41   Bend, Oregon

Bend, Oregon is a sportsman's paradise. Located in Central Oregon it's home to the Deschutes River and Mount Bachelor. It's a great place for hiking, biking, climbing, skiing, and fishing. And after a long day of doing your outdoor thing you can enjoy a burger and beer at the Deschutes Brewery.

Bend consistently ranks in the top 10 places to live and is a wonderful vacation destination.

After college, my friends and I skied Mt. Bachelor a few times and fell in love with Bend. My college roommate loved it so much he decided to pack his bags and move to Bend, and he has taken full advantage of all it offers. He has spent many hours fly fishing on the Deschutes, skiing Deadwood Canyon, and mountain biking on the Funner-Tiddlywinks trail.

As nice as Bend is, however, my friend has travelled the world looking for bigger fish, deeper powder, and longer trails. Whether fly fishing in Alaska, dove hunting in Argentina, or heli-skiing in Canada, he's taken the road less traveled and it has treated him well.

What does Bend have in common with investing?

Most investors never leave their home country when it comes to investing. They're satisfied with owning stocks in their backyard and not spending time exploring the four corners of the earth looking for new and fresh ideas. This creates a home country bias and it could be hazardous to your investment portfolio. According to a Vanguard study, investors held 27% of their assets in foreign companies. If investors were staying true to a global allocation, they should allocate about 50% of their assets overseas.[1]

In a recent study on diversification by Dimensional Fund Advisors, they highlighted the lost decade of 2000 to 2009. During this period, the S&P 500 lost 9.10% while the MSCI Emerging Markets Value Index was up 212.72%. Last year, the top three developed markets were Denmark, Belgium, and Japan, up 23.4%, 12.1%, and 9.6% respectively. The U.S. market returned .7%. Since 1996, the U.S. market had the best return twice – 2013 and 2014. The best returns for the other 18 years were found beyond our shores.[2]

You may live in an awesome city and own solid investments, but I'd recommend leaving your home port to explore opportunities far and wide.

In the beginning God created the heavens and the earth. ~ Genesis 1:1

May 14, 2016

Dow Jones = 17,710.71

---

[1] Dimensional Fund 2015 Matrix Book.

[2] Ibid.

42   Are Forest Fires Good?

The Yellowstone National Park fire of 1988 was one of the largest in U.S. history. It burned over 1 million acres and on "Black Saturday," the worst day of the fire, it consumed over 150,000 acres.[1]

This fire was devastating in terms of acreage burned and animals lost, but it also was a re-birth for the park. Fire is needed to clear out brush, dead trees, and other items so new life can begin to grow. Birds and bears returned to the burned area to nest and feed.

My family and I visited Yellowstone in 2004 and were awed by its beauty. We spent some time exploring the area burned by the fire. The once scorched earth was now covered with millions of trees. A park ranger told us not one tree was planted by human hands and the new trees were growing because of the fire. He mentioned the fact that for the seeds to open, they need heat like a popcorn kernel. If not for the fire, these trees wouldn't have taken root and grown.

A forest fire brings new life as will a stock market correction. Like a forest fire, a market correction isn't fun to experience, but it's needed for new growth. For a recovery to take hold there must be some destruction. When the market is falling it feels like the correction will never end. During a down draft is

---

[1] https://www.nps.gov/yell/learn/nature/1988fires.htm.

when panicked people abandon their investment strategy, not realizing better times are ahead.

According to The Reformed Broker, the average stock market correction results in a drop of 13.3% and lasts 71 days while a recovery lasts 221 days and has an average annual return of 32%.[2]

Let's look at some recent history. The Dow Jones rose 83% from the lows of the Tech Wreck in the early 2000s and climbed 6,339 points. Since the lows of the Great Recession in 2009, the Dow Jones Industrial average is up 148% and has climbed over 10,000 points. Investors who sold their stocks during the last two corrections missed these epic rebounds.

A study of stock market performance from 1970 to 2015 by Dimensional Fund Advisors found that investors who missed the 25 best up days saw a huge drop in their returns. A buy and hold strategy during this 45-year stretch turned a $10,000 investment into $89,678. If you missed the 25 best days during this run, your $10,000 grew to $21,224. By timing the market, you would've lost a lot of money. A $10,000 investment in U.S. T-Bills during this same period returned just $9,195.[3]

---

[2] http://thereformedbroker.com/2013/08/20/a-field-guide-to-stock-market-corrections/comment-page-19/, Joshua M. Brown, August 20, 2013.

[3] Dimensional Fund Advisors – Performance of the S&P 500 Index, 1970–2015.

What happened to Yellowstone a year after the fire? Visitors returned in droves. In 1989, attendance for the park reached a record for the decade, of over 2.6 million visitors![4]

Remember that a recovery always follows a correction so don't get burned by trying to time the market!

...*for our "God is a consuming fire." ~ Hebrews 12:29*

May 19, 2016

Dow Jones = 17,435.40

---

[4] http://www.ksl.com/?sid=26482639, Celeste Tholen Rosenlof, August 17, 2013.

43   The Graduate

It's an exciting time to be a college graduate. After years of tests and toils you're now ready to apply what you've learned in the classroom by taking it to the streets.

Here are a few thoughts to help guide you on your journey.

Think big. Somebody, somewhere, somehow is going to change the world. Why not you? You're more than qualified to be you and you can do amazing things. As Henry Ford said, "If you think you can do a thing, or you can't do a thing you're right." Now is the time to go big and make your mark on the world.

Think small. It would be nice to have a 10,000-square foot home with seven big-screen TVs, four refrigerators, a five-car garage and Olympic-size swimming pool, but you don't need it today. In fact, you don't need it at all. The more stuff you own the more shackled you'll be to your job, city, bank, etc. A smaller home with less stuff means more dollars in your pocket.

Think of others. In Mark 12:31, Jesus says to love your neighbor as you love yourself. If you put others first, you're likely to help yourself as well. Zig Ziglar said, "You can have everything in life you want, if you will just help enough other people get what they want."

Give. Get in the habit of giving away 10% of your pay to others. The Bible recommends giving a tithe, or 10%, of your first fruits. The more you give, the more you'll receive.

Save. Try to save 10% of your income. The amount you save should be deposited into a savings or money market account. Your savings account will allow you to put a down payment on a home or buy a new car. The more money you have in savings means the less you'll be dependent on others.

Invest. I recommend investing 10% of your pay in stocks of all shapes and sizes – large, small, and international. The sooner you start investing, the more money you'll have in the future. The stock market will be your BFF for the long-haul IMHO. The only way for you to reach your long-term financial goals is to be an owner of stocks. According to Dimensional Fund Advisors, a $1 investment in U.S. stocks from 1926 to 2015 is now worth $6,031. If you took the "safe" route and invested in U.S. T-Bills, your $1 is now worth $21.[1] Investing and saving are two different things, but both are needed for financial success.

Spend. If you've been doing the math, you're left with 70% of your income. Can you live on 70%? Now is the time to figure it out because once you have a house, a spouse, a few kids, a dog, a cat, a fish, you probably won't be able to live on 70%. Get in the habit now of spending less and saving more.

---

[1] Dimensional Fund Advisors 2015 Matrix Book.

Start your own company. In the gig economy, you can call your own shots. According to one study about 40% of the work force in 2020 will be working in the gig economy.[2] Besides, a big company will love you until it doesn't. In 2015, there were 493,431 announced layoffs through October 1, according to Challenger, Gray, and Christmas.[3] Now is the time to stick your flag in the ground and stake your claim.

Travel. It's a big planet out there. With a laptop and iPhone, you can work from New York, Paris, London, or Munich. You're as free as the wind, so take advantage of it.

Smile. A simple smile mixed in with a please and a thank you will open many doors for you. Don't be shy, spread a little cheer with your pearly whites.

Congratulations! Now go do some good.

Good habits formed at youth make all the difference. ~ Aristotle

May 23, 2016

Dow Jones = 17,492.93

---

[2] http://www.challengergray.com/press/press-releases/2015-october-job-cut-report-50504-cuts-over-13k-due-oil.
[3] Ibid.

44   Rates Are Rising! Buy Bonds?

The Federal Reserve raised interest rates in December and it might do it again in 2016. When interest rates rise, bond prices fall. The relationship is like a see-saw in a park: as one side rises, the other falls. If interest rates are going to rise, why would you want to buy bonds?

It's true a rate rise will cause a disruption in bond prices. It's in this turbulence where a bond buyer can find opportunity.

The 30-year U.S. Treasury Bond is currently paying 2.64%. A 1% rise in interest rates will reduce the price of this bond by 18%, falling from $100 to $81.92. A buyer of this bond at $81.92 can make 22% when it matures to $100. In addition, the current income jumped from 2.64% to 3.22% by buying it at $81.92.

Since 1926, the U.S. T-Bill has generated an average annual return of 3.4% while the long-term government bond has averaged 5.6%.[1]

Bond funds are considered lousy investments when interest rates rise. However, it's assumed, incorrectly, that the fund manager is doing nothing when rates are rising. In a rising rate scenario, she's buying bonds at lower prices while locking in higher rates.

---

[1] Dimensional Fund Matrix Book 2016.

The Franklin U.S. Government Securities Fund (FKUSX) is one of the oldest bond funds. Since May of 1970 it has delivered an average annual return of 6.26%. The best year was 1982, when it gained 33.04%. The worst year was 1980, when it lost 12.87%. A $100,000 investment in May of 1970 is now worth $1,624,990.[2]

When rates rise, the first reaction for bond holders is to sell. When they sell it creates a buying opportunity for individuals with a longer-term view. A buyer can take advantage of panic sells by buying bonds at favorable prices. Their pain will be your gain.

Why buy bonds when rates rise?

- Lower prices
- Higher coupons
- Better total return
- More choices

Don't fear the rate rise, it will treat you well in the long run.

The Chinese use two brush strokes to write the word "crisis." One brush stroke stands for danger; the other

---

[2] Morningstar Office Hypothetical Tool.

for opportunity. In a crisis, be aware of the danger – but recognize the opportunity. ~ John F. Kennedy

May 26, 2016

Dow Jones = 17,828.29

45   June Gloom

During the month of June, the beaches of Southern California are covered with a marine layer until mid-morning. From the pier in Huntington Beach to the jetty in Mission Beach, this haze hangs around until the sun powers through the clouds and exposes the beach goers to the glory of all California has to offer. This haze is referred to as the June Gloom.

On the beach you can often hear tourists grumbling about the overcast sky and cold weather. They're ready to take advantage of the spectacular coastline but some visitors get disgruntled and pack it in early, not knowing the sun is working its magic behind the scenes. This short-term thinking causes many to miss out on the sun and fun, while patient beach goers are rewarded with postcard weather.

Stocks, at times, are in a fog and this puts investors in a stubborn mood. The fog layer on the stock market will keep a lid on the upside until it burns off. The haze is habitually brought on by negative press coverage, faulty forecasts, "expert" opinions, analyst recommendations, or some other defective barometer.

In 2016, the average daily change in the S&P 500 was .04% or $4 for every $10,000 invested. Last year the average daily change was .01% or $1 for every $10,000.[1] These moves are

---

[1] Yahoo! Finance historical stock prices.

benign, and this lack of movement causes investors to make changes to their portfolio when none are needed.

A classic example of investors selling a stock for no reason is McDonald's. Last year it hovered around $95 from February to October. It was written off because it had apparently lost its way to several "new" burgers from trendier restaurants. Since October, MCD is trading at $124, up 30.5%. A move like that can pay for a lot of Happy Meals for the patient investor.

Facebook is another stock held back for one reason or another. It was trading around $75 from February 2014 to July 2015 before it shot up to $118, generating a gain of 57%.

Exxon was selling in the low $70s because the price of oil was supposed to trade lower. This gloom hung around from November 2015 to February before it rose to $90. Investors had pumped it up 21%.

These three stocks, and many more, were held back because of some type of haze. Individuals who get trapped in short-term trading miss out on long-term gains. When your stocks are under a cloud of uncertainty sometimes it pays to wait for it to burn off.

The end of a matter is better than its beginning, and patience is better than pride. ~ Ecclesiastes 7:8

June 1, 2016

Dow Jones = 17,789.67

46   The Five Best Ways to Run Out of Money

Regardless of how many zeros are in a paycheck, people tend to spend what they make and then some. The pitfalls listed here are easy to avoid because you can control many things, like spending and saving.

Here are the five best ways to run out of money:

No budget. Without a budget, it's impossible to get a handle on your spending. A budget will help you identify the good, the bad, and the ugly in your spending habits. What's the best way to prepare one? I recommend reviewing your credit card and bank statements to see where your money has gone. This initial review of your spending habits will give you the framework for your budget. You can also compare your spending to others with the Consumer Expenditure Survey found at www.bls.gov/cex.

Spending more than you make. If you make $1 and spend $2, you'll run into financial Armageddon. Are there items in your budget you can remove or eliminate? Let's say you're a foodie and eat out three times a week with an average restaurant tab of $100. At this pace you'd spend $14,400 on fine dining during the year. Cut your dining tab in half and invest the money at 7% and you could end up with over $312,000 in 20 years. The less you spend, the more you'll save.

Keeping up with the Joneses. If you're in an arms race with your neighbors, you'll lose. Do you need a bigger boat, faster car, or country club membership? A neighborhood country club membership may cost you $1,000 per month (golf, tennis, pool, food, tips, etc.). A 20-year member can spend over $328,000 on green fees and bacon-wrapped shrimp.

No savings. A lack of savings is upsetting. According to the Huffington Post, 73% of Americans can't cover six months of family bills.[1] Once your budget is finished, you'll be able to calculate how much you should invest in a savings account. I recommend six months of expenses. If you have access to cash, you can use it for emergencies and opportunities instead of relying on debt.

Too much debt. I've had more than a few people tell me they have no debt except for a home mortgage and a car loan. Even too much of this debt can bring down the house. According to the Motley Fool, credit card debt is $882 billion, auto debt $943 billion, student loan debt $1.2 trillion, and mortgage debt $8.13 trillion.[2] Big numbers. The less debt you owe the

---

[1] Jillian Berman, Associate Business Editor, Huffington Post, updated June 24, 2013,
http://www.huffingtonpost.com/2013/06/24/americans-savings_n_3478932.html.

[2] https://www.fool.com/investing/general/2015/01/18/the-average-american-has-this-much-debt-how-do-you.aspx, Todd Campbell (TMFEBCapital), January 18, 2015.

better your balance sheet will look. Your total debt payments should be no more than 38% of your gross income.

You can control how much you spend and save, and this is good news. Less of the former and more of the latter will put you on solid financial ground.

Neither a borrower nor a lender be… ~ Shakespeare's Hamlet

June 6, 2016

Dow Jones = 17,920.33

47   Boardwalk, Marvin Gardens, or St. James Place?

Monopoly is one of the best board games ever created. Who hasn't played Monopoly for hours trying to acquire Boardwalk, railroads, or hotels? My family has enjoyed playing it for years.

During the height of the depression, in 1935, Parker Brothers started marketing Monopoly nationwide and it became a huge hit. Millions of people found comfort playing the game during the dark days of the depression.

What can we learn from playing Monopoly?

Patience. A game of Monopoly can take hours, sometimes days. Like Monopoly, you need patience if you want to be a successful investor because it may take months or years for your stocks to turn into winners.

Diversification. It's impossible to win if the only property you own is Boardwalk. Rent for Boardwalk is $50. However, if you also own Park Place and put a hotel on it the rent soars to $2,000, an increase of 3,900%! In addition to prime places on the board, it helps to own railroads and utilities. Your portfolio should also be diversified so you can make money from multiple investments.

Cash flow. Collecting $200 when you pass Go is sweet. Passing Go is like receiving a dividend from a stock. A dividend is a gift that keeps on giving. According to Morningstar, there are 2,966 companies with a dividend that yields more than 3%.[1]

Small companies. Who wants to own Mediterranean Avenue? It's probably considered a small cap as far as Monopoly goes. Rent for this property is only $2. It's not much on the surface but it can add up over time. A hotel raises the rent to $250, which is devastating if you just passed Go and land on it. According to Dimensional Fund Advisors, a dollar invested in small company stocks in 1926 grew to $16,743 by the end of 2015. A dollar invested in Treasury Bills was worth $21.[2]

Taxes. It's never fun to land on the luxury or income tax square because they both take money out of your cash pile. Unfortunately, it's not possible to avoid taxes completely, but you can minimize them by investing in tax-free or tax-deferred accounts.

Expenses. The rent due for Electric Company or Water Works can be up to 10 times the amount shown on the dice. If you land on Water Works and roll boxcars the rent is going to cost $120. You shouldn't leave your family expenses to a roll of the dice. It's important to get a handle on your expenses and lower them as much as possible. The lower your expenses are, the larger your bank account will be.

Debt. I'm sure you've been in a marathon Monopoly match where someone, maybe you, has had to mortgage his

---

[1] Morningstar Office.
[2] Dimensional Fund Advisors 2015 Matrix Book.

property to survive. A player with mortgaged properties will eventually lose. The debt level on his properties will crush him. In real life, a high debt level will eventually crush you as well. The less debt you owe the more money you can invest.

Luck. We all need a little luck in life and investing. A "get out of jail free" card or "advance to go" card is something to cherish. Luck isn't a strategy and can't be quantified.

I'd rather be lucky than good. ~ Lefty Gomez

June 9, 2016

Dow Jones = 17,985.19

48 Beware of Falling Interest Rates?

Interest rates continue to fall with no floor in sight. Japan and Germany currently have negative rates while the yield on the five-year U.S. Treasury note is 1.05%. How can you take advantage of falling interest rates?

Here are a few suggestions.

Bonds. If you own bonds, you're likely sitting on capital gains. It may be worth it for you to sell some of them to lock in your gains. Let's say you purchased a bond paying 5% at a price of $100 a few years ago and today it's worth $105. You can sell your bond and lock in a $5 profit.

Refinance. It may be time to refinance your mortgage. According to Bankrate the 30-year fixed rate is 3.66%.[1] If you owe $300,000 on your home with a current mortgage rate of 5%, your monthly payment is $1,610.46. If you refinanced to 3.66%, your monthly payment drops to $1,374.07, saving you $236.38 per month or $2,836.56 per year.

Mortgage. If you still have a mortgage and you're sitting on a pile of cash, you should explore paying it off. By paying it off you'll increase your monthly cash flow and save money on the interest. For example, if after 10 years you decide to pay off your $300,000, 30-year mortgage with a 5% interest rate, you'll save $1,610 per month or $19,320 per year. In addition,

---

[1] Accessed June 15, 2016.

you'll save over $175,000 in interest by paying it off 20 years before it's due.

Gold. With near zero interest rates in the U.S. and negative rates overseas it may make sense to purchase gold coins. They can be used as a portfolio hedge and give you some exposure to alternative investments. In addition, they can be used as family heirlooms and passed down to future generations. The best place to purchase gold coins is directly from the United States Mint at www.usmint.gov. The current price of the American Eagle 2016 One Ounce Gold Proof Coin is $1,610.

Dividends. According to Morningstar, there are 192 companies currently yielding over 2% that have raised their dividend by 10% per year.

Preferred stocks. Allocating a portion of your fixed income portfolio to preferred stocks will give it a boost. There are currently two preferred stocks exchange traded funds yielding over 5.25%. PFF is the iShares Trust U.S. Stock ETF and PGX is the PowerShares Preferred Portfolio ETF.

Charity. Falling interest rates coupled with a large cash holding is a good recipe for giving money to others. A charitable donation to your church or favorite organization will help others and you'll receive a tax deduction for your generosity.

As interest rates continue to fall, look for ways to help others, reduce your expenses, or allocate your cash to higher yielding investments.

The man who had received five bags of gold went at once and put his money to work and gained five bags more. ~ Matthew 25:16

June 15, 2016

Dow Jones = 17,640.17

49   Fish and Chips

While visiting London a few years ago, I was excited to see Big Ben, Number 10 Downing Street, Tower of London, Westminster Abbey, and Buckingham Palace. These historical places lived up to their pre-trip hype, but what I was really looking forward to was eating a big helping of fish and chips.

In a couple of days, the residents of Britain will go to the polls and vote on Brexit. The vote will cause some market disruption and could be a bloody mess regardless of the outcome. With the pending vote, does it make sense to commit a portion of your account to international investments? Yeah, baby!

According to a recent report from Dimensional Fund Advisors, international markets account for 48% of the global market valuation, so it wouldn't be prudent to ignore half the world when it comes to constructing your portfolio. The UK accounts for 6.5% of the global market, sandwiched between Japan at 8.4% and Canada at 3.3%.[1]

Let's look at three Dimensional international mutual funds: DFA United Kingdom Small Company Fund, DFA International Portfolio, and the DFA Emerging Markets Portfolio.

---

[1] Dimension Fund Advisors, Global Equity Markets dated May 2016.

A $10,000 investment in the DFA United Kingdom Small Company Fund in March of 1986 is now worth $235,380. The 30-year average annual return for this fund has been 11%.[2]

A $10,000 investment in the DFA International Portfolio Fund in February of 1994 is now worth $34,499.[3]

A $10,000 investment in the DFA Emerging Markets Fund in April of 1994 is now worth $37,272.[4]

The key to long-term investment success is diversification. A portfolio of large, small, and international companies will allow you to take advantage of multiple markets. As the saying goes, diversification is the only free lunch on Wall Street!

Cheerio!

Do you know what's remarkable? Is how much England looks in no way like Southern California. ~ Austin Powers

June 21, 2016

Dow Jones = 17,829.73

---

[2] Morningstar Office Hypothetical Illustration Tool.
[3] Ibid.
[4] Ibid.

50 California, Texas, or Britain?

The Brexit vote has come and gone, with the citizens of the United Kingdom voting to leave the European Union. This sent shock waves through the global financial markets on Friday. The Dow Jones fell 3.3%, The Stoxx Europe 600 dropped 7%, and the Nikkei declined 7.9%. The Pound was pounded on Friday, falling almost 9% – its worst showing in over 31 years.[1] The UK is now a financial island both literally and figuratively.

What happens if California or Texas decided to leave the United States? It would be devastating because both states pack a powerful global punch.

California will never leave the United States. It accounts for 3.3% of the global GDP.[2] Fourteen of the largest companies in the world call it home.[3] Companies headquartered in the Golden State include Apple, Alphabet, Chevron, Disney, Gilead, QUALCOMM, and Wells Fargo. If California were a stand-alone country, it would rank seventh based on its GDP.

How about the Lone Star State? Texas is home to 16 of the largest companies, including AT&T, American Airlines, Exxon,

---

[1] http://money.cnn.com/2016/06/24/investing/pound-crash-eu-referendum/ Ivana Kottasova, June 24, 2016.

[2] http://www.bea.gov/iTable/drilldown.cfm?reqid=70&stepnum=11&AreaTypeKeyG..., accessed June 25, 2016.

[3] http://fortune.com/global500/ accessed June 25, 2016.

and Baker Hughes.[4] It accounts for 2.2% of the global GDP and if it were a country, it would rank 12th.

If California and Texas were combined into one country, it would account for 5.5% of the global GDP and be the fourth largest "country" in the world, sitting behind the U.S., China, and Japan. Thirty of the largest companies in the world would be included in this combined country.

The United Kingdom accounts for 3.8% of the global GDP.[5] Britain is home to 28 of the largest companies in the world.[6] The population of Britain is about 65 million, while the combined population of California and Texas is 66 million.[7] Britain is a global force, but a combined California and Texas is a bigger player on the global stage.

The markets reacted poorly to the outcome of Brexit mostly because it was caught off guard as bookies and pollsters had predicted Britain would remain in the EU. It's important to note that Britain isn't going away, nor will their companies stop producing goods and services. This transition will take years, maybe decades, before it's finalized.

In the meantime, use this event as an opportunity to reevaluate your international investments to see if they still make sense for your long-term goals. How much should you

---

[4] Ibid.
[5] https://en.wikipedia.org/wiki/Comparison_between_U.S._states_and_countries_by_GDP_(nominal), accessed June 25, 2016.
[6] http://fortune.com/global500/ accessed June 25, 2016.
[7] http://worldpopulationreview.com, accessed June 25, 2016.

allocate to international investments? According to Morningstar, this range can be as low as 5% or as high as 23%.

Last, the UK was formed over 300 years ago, so I think they'll be fine.

There is a time for everything, and a season for every activity under the heavens. ~ Ecclesiastes 3:1

June 25, 2016

Dow Jones = 17,140.24

51   My Week at a Dude Ranch

This past week my family and I spent our vacation at Wind River Ranch, a Christian dude ranch in Estes Park, Colorado. It's a magical place nestled in a valley between Longs Peak and Twin Sisters.

I spent time riding, hiking, and fishing while trying to act like a cowboy. These activities can teach us a lot about investing.

While riding horses through the Rocky Mountain National Park it was easy to get lost in my thoughts as I meandered along the trails. I had to remind myself I was sitting on a thousand-pound animal on a narrow trail and had to remain focused on where I was leading my trusted steed. I had to keep looking forward, so I wouldn't run into a tree or fall off a ledge. Riding a horse while looking over your shoulder is risky. Also, horses aren't too fond of walking backwards. So, too, with investing. It is imperative to keep moving forward towards your short- and long-term financial goals. Looking backwards to apply the coulda-shoulda-woulda strategy is a waste of time.

Hiking in the Rocky Mountain National Park is breathtaking. I hiked two trails. The first was a beautiful route along Glacier Creek to Mills Lake. It looked like a giant swimming pool on a windless day. The water was smooth as glass and clear as could be. The second hike was to the top of Twin Sisters with an elevation of 11,427. It wasn't a fourteener but challenging nevertheless – especially coming from the lowlands of Texas. On both hikes I needed to plan my route and make sure I had all my supplies, especially my bear bell. When you invest, it's important to be prepared for all types of conditions. A financial plan and investment strategy will help guide you to your financial goal. An asset allocation policy will allow your account to weather a storm or two. As in hiking, it's important to stop every now and then to make sure you're on the right trail and still marching towards your goal.

Fly fishing in the Rockies is about as good as it gets. Whether in rivers, streams, or crystal-clear lakes it's part art, part science. I used four or five different fly patterns and all of them worked at one level or another, some more than others. However, not every cast caught a trout. I spent a fair amount of time casting and waiting. I needed patience. Investing requires patience as well.

Whether you're hiking, riding, or fishing each requires a solid plan, the correct equipment, and constant monitoring to succeed. Investing also requires these attributes. The more you plan, the better your investment results will be.

Be still, and know that I am God; I will be exalted among the nations, I will be exalted in the earth. ~ Psalm 46:10

July 4, 2016

Dow Jones = 17,840.62

52   There's Gold in Them Thar Hills!

The California gold rush of 1849 brought millions of speculators to the Golden State in search of riches. A few made money but most lost everything. It appears there is another gold rush occurring today with the returns on gold turning in a stellar performance for 2016. In addition, silver is also having an epic run.

According to a recent Morningstar report, $4.1 billion was invested into precious metal funds last week – the most ever![1] Investors continue to chase the precious returns of gold and silver. With gold and silver shining this year does it make sense to make them a major holding in your portfolio? The short answer is no.

Gold is soaring, with the yellow metal up over 28% so far in 2016. The 30-year average annual return for gold has been 1.98%. A $10,000 investment in gold in 1986 is now worth $18,007. But the five-year average annual return generated a negative 4.27%.[2]

Silver usually plays second fiddle to gold, but not this year. It's up 42%. The five-year average annual return for silver has been a negative 13.5% per year. A $10,000 investment in silver

---

[1] http://news.morningstar.com/all/market-watch/TDJNMW20160708205/going-for..., Sara Sjolin, MarketWatch, July 8, 2016.
[2] http://www.macrotrends.net/1333/historical-gold-prices-100-year-chart, accessed July 7, 2016.

five years ago is now worth $4,842. The 30-year return for silver has been like the return on gold, with a 2% average annual return.[3] As a point of reference, inflation has averaged 2.6% since 1986.[4]

Why are these investments doing well? A big factor is fear. The world appears to be a little unsettled, and when fear and uncertainty are high gold and silver perform well. As investors focus on the headlines of Brexit, the police attacks in Dallas, and the election money continues to pour into gold and silver.

If you still have the gold bug and want to add precious metals to your account, limit your exposure to 3% or 5% of your account balance. If your investable assets are $1 million, your allocation to gold or silver can fall in the range of $30,000 to $50,000.

Choose my instruction instead of silver, knowledge rather than choice gold. ~ Proverbs 8:10

July 9, 2016

Dow Jones = 18,226.93

---

[3] http://www.macrotrends.net/1470/historical-silver-prices-100-year-chart, accessed July 8, 2016.
[4] US Inflation: Changes in US CPI Index 1926–2015, Dimensional Fund Advisors Matrix Book 2016.

53   Women and Poverty

Women are 80% more likely to end up in poverty than men according to a recent article in the *Austin American Statesman*.[1] A difference in pay is a major reason for this heartbreaking statistic. Women earn about 76 cents on the dollar when compared to the compensation for men.[2] This difference in pay over a 40-year career amounts to over $430,000.[3] Other factors tilting the scales against women are divorce and longevity.[4] Women are more likely to stay at home and raise children as well as be the caregivers for parents, taking them away from the workforce or severely reducing their working hours.

Whether you're married, divorced, single, or widowed, here are a few strategies to help strengthen your financial situation.

Create a budget. A budget will give you a picture of where your money is going. Mint.com is a tremendous resource for helping individuals get their financial life organized. Using your notebook to record cash purchases is a wise idea. Once cash leaves an ATM most people don't keep a list of how it's spent. It's easy to get nickeled and dimed with cash transactions. After a few months of tracking your expenses you should be

---

[1] "Older Women More Likely than Men to Face Poverty," Adam Allington, Associated Press, Austin American Statesman, July 11, 2016.
[2] Ibid.
[3] Ibid.
[4] Ibid.

able to identify an item or two to reduce or eliminate. Lower expenses result in more savings.

Create a financial plan. A financial plan will help quantify your hopes, dreams, and fears. It will expand your budget to include investments and liabilities. An annual review of your plan will keep your financial life on the right track. The best time to review it is near your birthday.

Automate your expenses. Automating your expenses will help your budgeting process and simplify your daily cash management activities. It may also improve your credit score as bills will always be paid on time. Automatic payments will also eliminate useless and expensive late fees.

Automate your investments. Setting up a monthly investment program into a savings account, mutual fund, or retirement account will allow you to create wealth automatically. The act of monthly investing is more important than the dollar amount. The money you save from your new budget can now be deposited into your investment accounts.

Establish an individual retirement account or IRA. The key to this account is the "I" which stands for individual. An IRA will be yours and yours only. If you're under 50 you can deposit $5,500 per year or 100% of your income if it's less than the maximum amount. If you're over 50, you can add an extra $1,000 to your account.

Get help. Working with a financial advisor, CPA, attorney, or banker can help you set up accounts, establish a budget or create an investment plan. A team of trusted advisors can help bring you financial tranquility.

Last, my Grandma Bee was born in 1900 and lived into her 90s. She always carried a small spiral notebook with a few colored pens in her purse. When I was young I would go shopping with her and after a purchase she would take out her notebook and jot down a few notes. I never knew what she was recording, but I'd like to think she was keeping track of her expenses. If it worked for my grandma, it will work for you too!

No one will be able to stand against you all the days of your life. As I was with Moses, so I will be with you; I will never leave you nor forsake you. ~ Joshua 1:5

July 12, 2016

Dow Jones = 18,347.67

54 Are We There Yet?

It's vacation time and millions of people are crisscrossing the country en route to their favorite destination. The top three U.S. destinations for this year are the Grand Canyon, Maui, and Yellowstone, according to U.S. News & World Report.

It's easy to know when you've arrived at your vacation destination because there's a big sign at the entrance welcoming you and your family. You probably spent months, maybe years, planning your adventure and you've invested time, energy, and dollars to make sure your trip is a success.

The key ingredient for a successful trip is the destination. Once you decide where to go, everything else falls into place. The end is now the beginning. When will you go? How will you get there? How long will you stay? What will you do? These are all questions you can now answer and with these inputs, you can now determine the cost of your trip.

Americans are good at planning a vacation but not so much when it comes to their retirement.

Retirement is an unknown journey. How do you know when you're ready to retire? Will there be a big sign at the entrance of your driveway informing you today is the day? Will it say you've arrived at your retirement destination? I doubt it.

Is it possible to calculate your financial needs for retirement? Yes. The first step is to calculate your household expenses. The next step is to multiply this number by 25. For example, if your expenses are $100,000 per year, you'll need assets of $2.5 million.

You may receive Social Security. It will lower the amount of money you'll need to save. If your Social Security is $30,000 per year, you can subtract it from your $100,000 in annual expenses to get $70,000. You now need assets of $1.75 million.

If you're fortunate enough to receive a pension, then it will lower the assets you need further. Let's say your annual pension is $25,000. Your annual expenses have been lowered by your Social Security and your pension. Your expense number is now $45,000 suggesting an asset level of $1.125 million.

It doesn't matter the age at which you obtain these assets because once you have them you can retire at any time.

To retire on your terms, you can lower your expenses or increase your assets. Are you there yet?

Life is either a daring adventure or nothing. ~ Helen Keller

July 19, 2016

Dow Jones = 18,559.01

55   A Runner's Guide to Retirement Planning

After years of running short races, I decided to run a marathon. My first one was the 1991 Los Angeles Marathon, and it was a disaster. On race day I thought I was ready for the 26.2-mile journey through LA.

I was young, naïve, and in shape, so the only strategy I had was to run as fast as I could for as far as I could. In short, I had no strategy. I was running without a plan.

My first miscalculation was my attire. I wore cotton, a major no-no for marathon runners. After a couple of miles, the shirt had to go. I took it off and ditched it on the side of the road, causing another problem. I was now shirtless and running without sunscreen. As the Southern California Sun bore down on me, I started to burn.

During the race, I avoided all the aid stations until mile 20. At this point I was done. I was dehydrated and sunburned. I started to walk but was saved by a young boy who gave me a giant bottle of Gatorade. His gift gave me enough fuel to get to the next aid station. The aid stations for the last 6.2 miles were of little use because I couldn't drink enough Gatorade to cure my thirst.

I finally finished the race and made it home where I could lick my wounds and reflect on the events of the day.

If I was going to continue to run marathons, I needed a plan. I read books on running and applied what I learned. My race experiences improved, and my times got faster. As a result, I qualified for the 2011 Boston Marathon and in 2015 I set a personal record in San Diego.

What does this have to do with retirement planning?

If you're a runner, you're most likely patient, disciplined, and goal oriented. Are you the same when it comes to planning your retirement? Do you spend as much time planning your retirement route as you do your running route?

Here are a few strategies to help get you to the retirement finish line with a smile on your face.

Plan. A sound retirement and financial plan will help guide your steps. It will align your investment holdings to your goals so they're both working for your benefit. The plan will give you a baseline of your current financial situation.

Think long term. A marathon is 26.2 miles, so don't worry about what's happening at mile 3 or 4. If you're retiring in 10, 20, or 30 years let your investments run and pay little attention to short term moves in the markets.

Find the right shoes. Running a marathon in high-quality, lightweight shoes makes all the difference in the world. So, too, when it comes to your investments. The "lighter" your fees the better your investment results. You can control your costs. When you're working on your financial plan you should also do a thorough review of your investment holdings. It's imperative to focus on low-cost funds and investments so you can drive your expenses lower.

Set your own pace. A large marathon may have 20, 30, or 40 thousand runners. It's likely you will pass, and get passed, by another runner during the race. Each runner in a race has her own goal, so don't get caught up trying to match her step for step. You'll be better served by focusing on your own goal and pace. Your retirement goals are yours only so don't try to keep up with the Joneses. Your financial plan will set your retirement pace.

Re-fuel and check in. Take advantage of all the aid stations on the race route. Taking a few seconds to hydrate and re-fuel will treat you well for the back half of the marathon. Once your retirement plan is up and running you'd be wise to check it every year to make sure you're still on pace to achieve your goals.

Run with a coach. Your running results may improve if you run with a coach. Who doesn't want a running partner or two when it's 5:00 in the morning and raining? Running with a group will help you stay focused and motivated. A financial coach or a team of trusted advisors can do the same. Your team will support you on your retirement journey. A financial coach can assist you with your financial decisions.

Go fast. Stocks will be your best friend during your retirement expedition. Stocks purchased for the long haul will help your assets grow faster than "safe" investments like bonds or cash.

When you cross the finish line stop running. The pain of the last few hours pales in comparison to the feeling you get when you cross the finish line. Your retirement plan will give you a finish line. If you've achieved the assets needed for your retirement, you can now afford to stop running and lock in your gains. Moving a portion of your investments to more conservative ones like bonds or cash can preserve your assets.

A plan for running and retirement can keep you going for a long time. I encourage you to get out there and start planning!

We all know that if you run, you are pretty much choosing a life of success because of it. ~ Deena Kastor

July 26, 2016

Dow Jones = 18,473.75

56 Playing with Legos

In the early 1970s I received my first Lego kit from my aunt and uncle. It was a small kit with few pieces and I played with it for hours. As I grew older my Lego collection expanded to thousands of pieces. A Lego set was to become my standard gift on special occasions.

To create a Lego masterpiece, it helps to have bricks of different shapes, sizes, and colors. The more pieces you own, the more complex your structure can be. Or not. Just because you have thousands of Lego pieces doesn't mean you should use them all. A simple Lego structure can work just as well as one with a lot of moving parts, maybe better.

The design of your investment portfolio, like your Lego structure, is only limited by your imagination. A well-diversified account is your best bet for long-term investment success.

In building your portfolio, focus on investments that will zig when others zag. The best indicator of how two or more investments will perform in your portfolio is the correlation coefficient. Two investments with a correlation of positive 1 will move in the same direction. Investments with a correlation of negative 1 will move in opposite directions. If one is up, the other is down.

Lego sets have changed dramatically from the early 1970s. With my limited choices, I could only build so many houses and forts. Lego sets today are mind boggling. A youngster can now build the Eiffel Tower, a Ferrari, Jurassic World, and a classic VW Bus.

Investments have also changed from the 70s. Then, investments were mostly limited to stocks and bonds. Mutual funds were just starting to gain popularity and exchange traded funds weren't yet on the horizon. Stock options became available for trading in 1974. Fees have also changed to the benefit of the investor. To buy a thousand shares of IBM 45 years ago, your commission would've cost you thousands of dollars. Today you can buy it without a commission.

Here are a few suggestions for how to construct your investment portfolio.

Diversify your investment holdings across asset classes. A portfolio of large, small, U.S., and international stocks mixed in with bonds, real estate, gold, and cash will allow you to participate in most market moves while reducing risk.

Focus on investments with low or negative correlations. A diversified account will have investments with high and low correlations, so make sure they're spread out across different asset classes.

Keep your fees low. Today, you can own a low-cost investment portfolio with individual investments or funds from Vanguard and Dimensional Funds. The lower your fees, the higher your returns.

If you're happy with your portfolio masterpiece, stop building. A portfolio should be built for the long haul and designed to stand the test of time.

Review your accounts occasionally. A quick look and review is needed to make sure your investments are performing well and still in line with your financial goals.

Last, be patient when building your investment portfolio. A Lego sculpture of quality takes time and thought, but once completed it's a thing of beauty. So, too, with your accounts!

Therefore everyone who hears these words of mine and puts them into practice is like a wise man who built his house on the rock. ~ Matthew 7:24

August 4, 2016

Dow Jones = 18,352.05

57   BUY, BUY, BUY, SELL, SELL, SELL…

CNBC is an excellent resource for following the stock market. It's like a combination of 60 Minutes, ESPN, and Jerry Springer. While I'm at work, I have it on in the background but listen to it with a heavy set of filters.

CNBC is a news channel with anchors jumping from story to story in rapid-fire succession, giving the viewer a constant account of the markets. The best (worst?) part of CNBC is when guests square off against each other to battle over the market, the economy, or a stock pick. The opposing parties attack and talk over each other while trying to convince the audience their opinion is right.

On any given day, you may hear hundreds of stock recommendations. These recommendations aren't selected for you but for their audience. The producers of the show don't care if you buy Amazon or Zillow. They want you to watch their show so they can sell more advertising.

It's rare to hear an anchor or commentator tell you to purchase low-cost index funds based on your personal financial plan and hold them forever. The buy and hold index investor gets little love from CNBC. The active trading hedge fund manager probably sells more advertising than a buy and hold passive index fund manager. Does this make sense? According to S&P's SPIVA® U.S. Scorecard over a 10-year investment time horizon 82% of large-cap fund managers,

87% of mid-cap fund managers, and 88% of small-cap fund managers underperformed their corresponding benchmarks.[1]

News travels faster than you can trade. By the time you hear news about your favorite stock, the market has already reacted and it's impossible for you to enter an order fast enough, so don't bother. The best thing for you to do when your stock is mentioned on CNBC is nothing. If it's mentioned, take time to review the headline and do your own homework before you react.

Don't buy a stock just because it's highlighted on CNBC. The people on CNBC know nothing about your personal financial situation, so if you feel compelled to act on their advice it's best to count to 10 and then call your advisor, who's familiar with your portfolio.

Fear sells, and down markets make big headlines. When the market is going down, which is normal, panic mode sets in and the anchors want to know if this is the beginning of the end. Market drops appear to pick up steam because of their broadcasts. I've yet to see a fire put out with kerosene.

CNBC can be a valuable tool if used correctly. It's a news channel, so use it accordingly and always default to your

---

[1] 2015 SPIVA® U.S. Scorecard, S&P Dow Jones Indices, Aye M. Soe, CFA, Senior Director, contributor.

financial plan. Do not make any rash decisions because BUY, BUY BUY is usually replaced with SELL, SELL, SELL.

Where there is no vision, the people are unrestrained, but happy is he who keeps the law. ~ Proverbs 29:18

August 10, 2016

Dow Jones = 18,495.66

58   Market Top. Now What?

The Dow Jones, S&P 500, and the Nasdaq all hit record highs yesterday. The last time this occurred was in 1999. I'm thankful and nervous to hear this news, because after the stock market peaked in 1999 it corrected in 2000. With markets trading at all-time highs what's an investor to do? After all, if you climbed a mountain and reached the peak your next move is to turn around and descend. Sir Edmund Hillary and Tenzing Norgay spent about 15 minutes atop Mount Everest before they headed for home.

A climber who's descending is rewarded with vistas not afforded while ascending. The descent allows the climber to reflect on the climb and focus on the next mountain. When the next stock market correction arrives, use it as an opportunity to identify new companies or sectors to add to your portfolio. A market drop will allow you to buy quality companies at fabulous prices.

As the market crests let's review previous tops to see what would have happened to your investment returns had you purchased stocks at the top of the market cycle.[1]

August 1, 1987–July 31, 2016. If you purchased stocks at this peak, your average annual return was 9.27%.

---

[1] Morningstar Office Hypothetical Tool. The returns are calculated with an ending date of July 31, 2016.

January 1, 1994–July 31, 2016. This market top purchase averaged 9.16% per year.

December 1, 1999–July 31, 2016. This investment produced an average annual return of 4.67%.

October 1, 2007–July 31, 2016. A 6.2% average annual return is what you earned after buying this market top.

February 1, 2015–July 31, 2016. The purchase of stocks a year and a half ago rewarded you with an average annual return of 8.21%.

An average of these averages is 7.5%. A 7.5% average annual return for buying at the "worst" time is impressive. Had you purchased bonds at these same peak levels, you generated an average annual return of 5.11%. If you kept your money in cash at these peak levels your return was .25% per year. A $100,000 investment earning 7.5% for the next 20 years will be worth $424,785. At 5.11% it will grow to $270,944. A 20-year investment earning .25% will be worth $105,120.

The urge to sell your stocks at a top is strong for most investors. I encourage you to fight this impulse to dramatically reduce your stock holdings and move to cash. Instead, focus on your long-term goals and investment plans.

Let the mountains bring peace to the people, And the hills, in righteousness. ~ Psalm 72:3

August 12, 2016

Dow Jones = 18,576.47

59   Money Follows the Heart

Creating a budget is about as fun as getting your wisdom teeth pulled, and most people would rather do anything else than figure out where their money is going. However, to be a successful investor, it's imperative to spend some time reviewing your spending habits.

According to the American Psychological Association, 72% of Americans say money is the number one cause of stress.[1] This is usually the result of not having a good handle on how their money is being spent.

The best way to create a budget is to spend time reviewing your credit card and bank statements from the past three to six months. January and July are ideal months to sit down and stroll through your finances. A January review will give you insight into your spending habits from the past year, while a July review will allow you to explore the previous six months of the current year. A useful resource to help you get a handle on your spending is Mint.com. After you've dissected your statements you should be able to identify places in your spending where you can make a few changes.

The breakdown of your spending habits will also tell you where your heart is, because people only spend money on things they need or want. Food, gas, and electricity are

---

[1] http://www.apa.org/news/press/releases/2015/02/money-stress.aspx, accessed August 14, 2016.

necessities while entertainment and hobbies are wants. Where does your money go?

According to the Bureau of Labor Statistics Consumer Expenditure Survey, here is where consumers spend their money. The numbers below are a percentage of your income. For example, Americans spend 12.6% of their income on food. If you earned $50,000, you spent $6,300 per year on food items.[2] How do you compare to the national average?

- Food = 12.6%
- Housing = 33%
- Property taxes = 3.6%
- Utilities = 7.3%
- Transportation = 17%
- Healthcare = 5.4%
- Entertainment = 5.2%
- Cell phones = 1.8%
- Reading = .2%

In 2015, Americans gave $373.2 billion to charities, or $2,974 per household. The three largest categories for giving last year were religion, education, and human services.[3] A suggested amount for giving is 10% of your income.

---

[2] http://www.bls.gov/cex/2014/combined/age.pdf, accessed August 13, 2016.
[3] https://www.nptrust.org/philanthropic-resources/charitable-giving-statistics/.

Also, if you don't know where your money is going, how do you know how much to save? A person with a spend first, save second mentality will never have enough money at the end of the month to invest. If you save first and spend second, your assets will continue to grow. How much should you save? As much as you can but at least 10% of your gross income. Your savings can be done through a corporate retirement plan in addition to your personal savings. Automating your monthly investing and spending will improve your financial outlook. The ability to transfer from your checking or savings account to an investment account or IRA is easy and routine.

With technology and the resources available to you today, it has never been easier to create a budget – yeah! Once you spend some time creating your budget, the review and maintenance of it will become second nature. After you figure out where your money has been going, you can turn your spending into savings!

For where your treasure is, there your heart will be also. ~ Luke 12:34

August 15, 2016

Dow Jones = 18,636.05

60 Marcia, Marcia, Marcia!

Eve Plumb, AKA Jan Brady, recently made headlines for selling her Malibu beach house for $3.9 million after buying it for $55,300 in 1969. A tidy profit for sure.

I'm a child of the 70s and grew up with a heavy dose of *The Brady Bunch*. If you grew up watching it, I'm sure you can recall almost any episode at a moment's notice. To this day people are still enamored with this classic sitcom.

Ms. Plumb did well with her investment. How can you go wrong buying Malibu beach-front property? It's probably one of the shrewdest investments one can make. The return on her investment, before taxes, was 9.4% per year. It performed well because she found value in her home and owned it for four decades. She probably could have sold it many times before and made a decent profit. However, generational thinking is needed to make a substantial profit.

What if she had invested her money in the stock market instead of buying the beach house? Let's look at a few investment alternatives.

A $55,300 investment in the S&P 500 index in 1969 produced an average annual return of 9.8%, giving her $4.47 million today.[1] It would've put an extra $570,000 into her pocket.

---

[1] Dimensional Fund Advisors Matrix Book 2016.

The same dollar investment in the Investment Company of America (AIVSX) 47 years ago is now worth $6.9 million, generating an average annual return of 10.79%.[2] This investment would've given her an extra $3 million.

A similar purchase of the Fidelity Magellan Fund (FMAGX) is now worth $15.63 million, averaging a 12.73% annual return![3] This investment delivered an extra $11.73 million! That's a lot of sand dollars.

What can we learn from Ms. Plumb's purchase?

- She did well with her real estate purchase because she found value in her investment. If you find value in your investments, you're more likely to hold on to them for a long time.
- She probably bought the home because of its location and the enjoyment it would bring to her and her family. I'm positive she didn't purchase the property at age 11 thinking in four decades she would sell it for a nice profit.
- Time wins. The best way to create wealth is to look to the horizon. Think long term and don't get spooked or sidetracked by short-term

---

[2] Morningstar Office Hypothetical Tool.
[3] Ibid.

thinking. A short-term, trader's mentality will leave your bank account with fewer dollars.
- Real estate owners do well because most people don't flip homes like they do stocks. They do well because of their long-term thinking. Stock investors should follow the lead of Ms. Plumb and other successful real estate investors and expand their investment timeline.
- Stocks win in the end. The long-term performance of quality stocks is hard to beat. If you want the opportunity to grow your wealth, add stocks to your portfolio.

For the record, I would've made the same investment choice as Ms. Plumb. What 11-year-old wants a portfolio of stocks?

When it was time to leave, we left and continued on our way. All of them, including wives and children, accompanied us out of the city, and there on the beach we knelt to pray. ~ Acts 21:5

August 20, 2016

Dow Jones = 18,529.42

61 My, How Time Flies!

Last week I helped my daughter move into her college dorm room. It was a rush of emotions as my thoughts drifted from college-bound freshman to tiny infant. Eighteen years flew by much faster than I thought possible. It seems like yesterday I was teaching her how to swim and ride her bike and in a blink of an eye she's a college student.

Time marches on and waits for no one. It's equal for all and it doesn't discriminate. Procrastination will cost you dearly when raising a child or saving for retirement.

When my daughter was born I couldn't wait to get her Social Security number, so I could open her college savings account, a Uniform Trust to Minors Account (UTMA). The UTMA allows for the purchase of stocks, bonds, and mutual funds. A 529 Plan allows you to invest in mutual funds based on your risk tolerance or your child's age and the money will grow tax free if it's used to pay for college.

Parents of a child born today can expect to spend $300,000 for their child to attend a four-year public university. If their child attends a private university, they can expect to pay twice that amount. The parents of a newborn have 18 years to save for college. If they start saving today they'd have to invest $8,823 per year to meet this goal. If they waited 10 years to start saving for college, their annual savings amount rises to $29,240 per year, an increase of 231%!

In 18 years from today, a 49-year-old worker will turn 67, the normal retirement age for many when it comes to collecting Social Security benefits. A 49-year-old may think she has many years to save for a comfortable retirement, but this isn't the case. Let's say she has $250,000 in a retirement account with a saving goal of $1 million in 18 years. If she earns 7% on her investments, she must save $4,559 per year to hit her target. Waiting 10 years to start saving money for this goal will now cost her $55,600, an increase of 1,119%!

What can you do if you have not started saving for college or funding your retirement? Is it possible for you to make up for lost time? Let's look at some options you can employ today to give your savings a passing grade.

Start saving today. It's imperative to start saving any amount you can towards your college and retirement goal. The longer you wait, the more you must save.

Automate your savings. If you establish an automatic link from your checking account to your college and retirement accounts, you're more likely to remain committed to your goal.

Buy stocks. An allocation to stocks will give your money the best opportunity to grow when compared to bonds or cash. The historical growth rate of large company stocks from 1926 to 2015 has been 10% per year.[1]

---

[1] Dimensional Fund Advisors Matrix Book 2016.

College or retirement? What if you must make a choice between saving money for college or saving money for retirement? Well, retirement wins. It's possible to get a loan or a scholarship for college but you can't get one for retirement.

When caught in the daily grind of life it's easy to lose focus of the future. On the surface 18 years seems like a long time from now. But it's not. Today you're holding your child in your arms and tomorrow your dropping her off at college. If you're in your 20s, 30s, or 40s, don't wait to start saving your money because 18 years will fly by in a blink of an eye!

Why, you do not even know what will happen tomorrow. What is your life? You are a mist that appears for a little while and then vanishes. ~ James 4:14

August 20, 2016

Dow Jones = 18,529.42

62   Five Rings. Five Things.

The Rio Olympics recently ended with the athletes and host country putting on quite a show. The Summer Olympics occur every four years and for a moment in time most of the world stops to root for their home country.

Here are five things I learned while watching the Rio Olympic Games.

All athletes are created equal, but some are more equal than others. Michael Phelps, Simone Biles, and Usain Bolt are in a class all to themselves. The level of athleticism and dominance they displayed in Rio is beyond parallel. The other athletes are also phenomenal and sometimes the distance between winning a gold medal or a silver one is less than 1/100th of a second. In your investment portfolio, you may own two or three stocks that are superior to your other holdings. A diversified portfolio of stocks will have many good companies. But a few of them are outstanding and produce returns well above the rest. These few can turn a mediocre year into an incredible one. If you're fortunate enough to own a few of these superior companies, it's best to let them run so they can continue to produce amazing results.

Two are better than one. Abbey D 'Agostino and Nikke Hamblin weren't household names prior to the Olympics. During the 5,000-meter qualifier they got tangled on a turn and fell and then helped each other to the finish line. These two young ladies exemplified the Olympic spirit and they'll forever be recognized for their sportsmanship. We all stumble from time to time as do our investments. What's important is that we get back up to finish the race. A diversified portfolio will own tens, hundreds, or thousands of investments and this will help you in the event one of them stumbles or falls.

Athletes train their whole lives for an opportunity to achieve Olympic glory. Sprinters train for thousands of hours to run the 100-meter race in less than 10 seconds. High jumpers, long jumpers, and pole vaulters practice repeatedly until they know the exact distance and timing needed to complete their jumps. Lionel Messi said it took him 17 years and 114 days to become an overnight success. To achieve investment success, it helps to think long term. It may take years before you start to see gold medal results from your investment efforts.

A few bad apples can spoil the whole bunch. Four swimmers from the United States embarrassed the host country, the U.S. Olympic Committee, their teammates, their home country, and themselves for fabricating a story about being robbed at gun point. Their story cast a pall over the Olympics because their foolish actions diverted attention from the glory of the games. These four should've told the truth from the beginning, or at least cut their losses when they realized they were in over their heads. A bad investment can bring down your entire portfolio if you let it become a distraction. It doesn't make sense to pour good money after bad. So, when you have an investment performing poorly it's best to cut your losses and move your money into a company that may provide you with a better return. A losing stock position will take your eyes off the rest of your account and you'll lose focus (and maybe sleep) worrying about the poor performer. Be honest with yourself when reviewing your holdings. Do you need to come clean with some of your losers?

The five Olympic rings represent the five continents. They're interlocking to symbolize a united world. The Olympics are designed to bring the world together for a few weeks every four years. They're a nice reminder of what a peaceful world looks like when the athletes march into the stadium during the opening ceremonies. Charitable giving and philanthropic strategies should be included in your investment and financial plan. Can your resources help others? Do you have assets you can donate to your favorite charity? A review of your investment holdings and personal goals may encourage you to provide gold to the people you assist.

The Summer Olympics are over, so now is a good time to review your investments to see if they can perform faster, higher and stronger.

I can do all this through him who gives me strength. ~ Philippians 4:13

August 28, 2016

Dow Jones = 18,502.99

63   Happy Birthday National Park Service!

The National Park Service celebrated its 100th birthday on August 25, 2016. President Woodrow Wilson signed the act forming the NPS. John Muir, Marjory Stoneman Douglas, Enos Mills, Charles Young, and Theodore Roosevelt were early pioneers in creating the NPS.[1] Yellowstone was established as the first national park in 1872, and the rest, as they say, is history.[2] Today the NPS includes over 400 areas in the United States covering 84 million acres.[3] There are currently 58 national parks from Acadia to Zion.

Ansel Adams introduced millions of people to the parks through his amazing black and white photographs of Half Dome, the Snake River and other storied locations. Last year, 305 million visitors visited at least one of our country's beautiful parks.[4]

My family and I have been to several National Parks over the years – Yosemite, Yellowstone, Grand Teton, Joshua Tree, Assateague Island, and the Rocky Mountain National Park. One of our favorite hikes was to Sentinel Dome in

---

[1] https://www.nps.gov/bestideapeople/, accessed September 1, 2016.
[2] Ibid.
[3] https://www.nps.gov/aboutus/history.htm, accessed September 1, 2016.
[4] https://www.nps.gov/aboutus/news/release.htm?id=1775, accessed September 1, 2016.

Yosemite. Once atop the dome we were treated to a 360-degree view of the park.

We should all applaud the vision and foresight of the early founders and leaders of the National Park System because their decisions have benefited legions of visitors. The NPS was forged with no end date, a perpetual objective.

When planning your future, it's imperative to think long term, as short-term thinking will derail most investment plans. With 24/7 access to news, it's easy to get spooked out of your investments and seek shelter in safe products. When establishing your plan, it would be wise to follow the trail of John Muir and the others.

How can you think long term?

Think about your family. Investing for generational wealth shifts your focus from short- to long-term thinking. Buying stocks for your grandchildren's children will allow your investments to grow and develop over time. A Sequoia tree grows for hundreds of years before it reaches maturity.

Avoid making investment decisions during market hours. If you hear news about your holdings, don't react. It's best to review your investments after market hours so you don't feel the urge to trade. Doing research at night or on the weekend will give you time to make thoughtful decisions. Of course, if you decide to buy or sell you must make the trade when the market is open, but you can do this after you've done your homework.

Review your financial plan and investment goals on a consistent basis. A return to your roots will remind you why you're investing in the first place.

Focus on charity. A gift to the National Parks or your favorite charity will allow your investment to benefit others. The return on this investment is priceless.

Our National Parks are treasures for all to explore. Here's a link to the NPS website so you can use it to find a park in your state: https://www.nps.gov/index.htm.

The mountains are calling and I must go. ~ John Muir

September 1, 2016

Dow Jones = 18,419.30

64   Dude, Where's My Car?

Getting a car fixed isn't fun. When my "check engine" light comes on, my blood pressure rises. A flat tire, cracked windshield, or an engine failure requires a visit to the automotive shop. One of my best friends from high school has been fixing cars for as long as I can remember. His nickname was MacGyver because he could fix anything. Brian opened Brian Wood Automotive several years ago and has successfully fixed cars for over 22 years.

To my knowledge, no one has ever driven his car to Brian's shop because nothing was wrong with it. People don't give their cars much thought if they're running well because they're expected to perform without incident. But it's nice to know it can be fixed if it did break down.

The stock market, of course, goes up and down. Like Brian, I don't receive calls from clients or investors when things are going well in the stock market. When it's up most people don't call to ask what's going right because it's always expected to rise. When it's "broken" or going down the phone rings off the hook. What's "wrong" with the stock market? Why is it falling?

Over the past five years the Standard & Poor's 500 stock index has increased over 78%. During this span, it has risen 54% of the time and fallen 46% of the time. The best up day during this stretch was November 30, 2011, when it rose 4.15%. The worst day was August 24, 2015, when it dropped 4.10%. The market had 20 days when it climbed 2% or more and 32 days when it fell 2% or more. From August 20, 2015 to August 25, 2015 the S&P 500 declined 10.92% to a level of 1,867.61. However, since the drop it gained 15% to a current level of 2,148.94. An investor who sold during the rout missed the 15% recovery.[1]

Brian is a successful business owner because he listens to his client, identifies the problem, and fixes the car. He encourages his customers to regularly maintain their vehicles to avoid bigger mechanical issues.

What can an investor learn from Brian Wood Automotive?

- Identify the problem in your portfolio and get it fixed.
- Review and maintain your portfolio so you can enjoy long-term returns from the stock market.
- Re-balance your tires and your portfolio.
- A financial plan is your diagnostic road map to keep your portfolio moving forward.

If everyone is moving forward together, then success takes care of itself. ~ Henry Ford

September 19, 2016

Dow Jones = 18,120.17

---

[1] https://finance.yahoo.com/quote/%5EGSPC?p=^GSPC, accessed September 19, 2016.

65   12 Reasons to Hire a Robo-Advisor

The robo-advisor market is booming with billions of dollars flowing into these programs. According to Cerulli Associates, the assets managed by robo-advisors will rise to $489 billion by the year 2020.[1] That's a lot of binary digits! I'm a fan of new technology and can't imagine life without my remote, microwave, or iPhone. I'm also a fan of robo-advisors.

How do you know if you're ready for a robo-advisor? Here are twelve signs you're ready to commit to a robo.

1. Your financial plan is complete. Your finished financial plan is giving you a clear path to your financial future and has helped you establish your asset allocation, savings goals, and asset targets.

2. Your estate plan is complete. Your family will or trust is up to date and all your children are listed by name. Your estate plan identifies your healthcare directives and recognizes your end-of-life wishes. Your family also knows where you keep your estate planning documents.

3. If you're retired you have an income distribution policy. Your income distribution plan lets you know how much money

---

[1] https://www.cnbc.com/2016/07/25/robo-advisors-may-have-too-much-control-over-your-portfolio.html, By Tom Anderson, July 26, 2016.

you can extract from your accounts each year so you'll never run out of money.

4. Your charitable and philanthropic plan is in force and your giving goals are well defined.

5. You're maxing out your annual 401(k) or company retirement plan contributions. A person under the age of 50 can contribute $18,000 per year while an individual over the age of 50 can add another $6,000 for a total of $24,000.

6. The beneficiaries on your retirement accounts and life insurance policies are current.

7. Your cash management is secure, and you have six months or more of household expenses in a checking, savings, or money market fund. If your monthly household expenses are $10,000, your emergency fund should be worth $60,000.

8. Your debt and liabilities are under control. The suggested debt payments for your household should be less than 38% of your gross income. If your monthly gross income is $10,000, then your total debt payments should be less than $3,800.

9. If you have children, your education plans are completely funded. The current annual cost for a private university is $47,381 while a public university is $24,061.

10. You own an adequate amount of life insurance. Your life insurance coverage will benefit your beneficiaries, eliminate your debt obligations, or pay for your children's college education.

11. You're familiar with the efficient market hypothesis and modern portfolio theory. You're a stout believer in the long-term appreciation of stocks and you won't panic over the market's gyrations.

12. You don't need any guidance with your investments or planning and you have no desire to talk to a human being.

If you're able to check these boxes, you're ready to move forward with a robo.

This mission is too important for me to allow you to jeopardize it. ~ HAL

September 22, 2016

Dow Jones = 18,392.46

66   5 Lessons from Vin Scully

The iconic Los Angeles Dodgers broadcaster, Vin Scully, is retiring from the broadcasting booth after 67 years! Mr. Scully had an amazing run broadcasting some of the best games in baseball history. I was fortunate to grow up in Los Angeles in the shadows of Dodger Stadium. The Dodgers of my youth had quite a run and even won the World Series the year I was born. My friends and I loved going to Dodger Stadium to watch the game and eat Dodger Dogs.

What can we learn from Mr. Scully's improbable and impossible career? Here are five takeaways.

Goals and dreams matter. According to Mr. Scully, he fell in love with baseball at the age of eight while watching the 1936 World Series. He had a goal and a plan to become a baseball announcer. To become a successful investor, you must have a plan. Your plan should outline your hopes, dreams and fears. The financial plan you create ought to carry you through all the innings of your life.

Sometimes nothing is something. Mr. Scully was the master of silence, especially when the crowd would roar to life as it did during Kirk Gibson's epic home run in the 1988 World Series. What more could he have added to the story? He once said, "I try to call the play as quickly as I possibly can and then shut up and let the crowd roar because, to me, the crowd is the most wonderful thing in the whole world when it's making noise."[1] Does it make sense to be an active trader darting in and out of the market? According to Dimensional Fund Advisors from 1970 to 2015, the S&P 500 Index generated an average annual return of 10.27%. If you missed the best 25 days during this 45-year span your average annual return dropped to 6.87%.[2] It makes sense, at times, to be patient and do nothing. Don't put yourself in a pickle, stay with the market!

Success takes a long time. Mr. Scully is a Hall of Fame broadcaster, living legend, and standard for all broadcasters. He's at the top of the list for the greatest broadcasters of all time. The broadcasting booth at Dodger Stadium is named after Mr. Scully and Vin Scully Boulevard runs from Sunset Blvd. to Dodger Stadium. Was he always the best? I'm sure he was good when he started broadcasting games at age 22, but it took years for him to go from good to great to immortal. What if you invested $10,000 in the Investment Company of America mutual fund (AIVSX) on opening day of 1950? At the end of August 2016 your $10,000 investment is now worth $17.2 million![3] And that, folks, is a lot of peanuts! Investing success also takes a long time.

---

[1] http://www.chicagotribune.com/business/columnists/ct-rosenthal-vin-scull..., Phil Rosenthal, Chicago Tribune, May 27, 2016.
[2] Reacting Can Hurt Performance, Dimensional Fund Advisor Investor Discipline Presentation, accessed September 26, 2016.
[3] Morningstar Office Hypothetical Tool.

He was prepared. If you've seen a picture of his desk, it's covered with notes upon notes.[4] His broadcasting style was smooth and effortless because of his tireless preparation. To be a successful investor you need to be prepared. You must do your homework before investing whether you invest on your own or work with a registered investment advisor.

He was humble and gracious. His focus was never on himself. He always gave credit to others and never wanted to be bigger than the game. While calling his last Dodger game he wanted the emphasis to be on the players. To be a successful investor you must respect the market and check your ego at the door because pride comes before the fall.

In a year that has been so improbable, the impossible has happened. ~ Vin Scully

September 27, 2016

Dow Jones = 18,228.30

---

[4] http://www.sportsonearth.com/article/62217474, Chuck Culpepper, September 30, 2013, accessed September 26, 2016.

67 Ten Thousand Men of Harvard

Harvard is a bastion of knowledge, a pillar of higher education and a fortress for the educational elite. John Adams, FDR, JFK, and George W. Bush have walked the Old Yard. Bill Gates, Tommy Lee Jones, and Ralph Waldo Emerson may have slept in Hollis, Grays, or Weld Hall. Harvard consistently ranks number one in most, if not all, educational categories.

The Harvard endowment fund managed by the Harvard Management Company is nothing to sneeze at. It's a behemoth, with assets north of $35 billion. And it has done well over time. According to the Harvard Management Company, the fund has averaged a 10% average annual return over the past 20 years.[1] However, its last fiscal year didn't go well. The fund suffered a loss of 2%, underperforming their benchmark by 3%.[2] Its posted five-year average annual return ending in June of this year was .5%.[3] Harvard is blessed with educational fire power and financial resources, so you'd think its endowment would be able to outperform the markets on a regular basis.

---

[1] http://www.hmc.harvard.edu/investment-management/performance-history.html, accessed September 28, 2016.

[2] http://www.hmc.harvard.edu/docs/Final_Annual_Report_2016.pdf.

[3] Ibid.

However, Harvard isn't alone in this camp of underachievers. A single financial institution, Long Term Capital, almost brought the financial world to its knees in 1998. While its management team included some Harvard alumni it also employed alums from MIT, Stanford, and the University of Chicago plus two Nobel Laureates.

The resources of Goldman Sachs, Morgan Stanley, Bridgewater Associates, Blackrock, and Citadel are unparalleled. Besides managing trillions of dollars, they hire the finest minds the Ivy League has to offer. Their employees, many with PhDs, constantly search for the needle in the haystack with algorithms and quant models running 24/7 looking for an investment edge, a luxury not afforded to Farmer John.

Underperformance of active money managers is nearly ubiquitous. According to Morningstar's Active/Passive Barometer Mid-Year 2016 Report, 93% of large cap money managers failed to survive 10 years and outperform their passive benchmark.[4]

What if, instead, you owned the entire haystack? Who cares if you never find the needle? I'd rather have the whole bale of hay anyways. In financial terms, the haystack is the stock market. Let's say you own the following five Vanguard Exchange Traded Funds: S&P 500 (VOO), Mid Cap (VO), International (VXUS), Real Estate (VNQ), and Bonds (BND). This

---

[4] Morningstar Active/Passive Barometer, August 2016, Ben Johnson and Alex Bryan.

equally weighted portfolio delivered a one-year return of 11.15%.[5] The five-year average annual return for this haystack portfolio averaged 10.25%! In addition to superior returns, your fees would've been a microscopic .09%.[6]

As you look to invest your hard-earned cash, my suggestion is for you to send your kid to Harvard and your money to an index fund!

Red, I should have been a farmer. ~ Pop Fisher, The Natural

September 29, 2016

Dow Jones = 18,143.45

---

[5] Morningstar Office Hypothetical Tool – August 31, 2015 to August 31, 2016.
[6] Morningstar Office Hypothetical Tool – August 31, 2011 to August 31, 2016.

68 "Mr. Speaker, The President of the United States!"

The elections are coming! On November 8th, Americans will go to the polls to elect the 45th President of the United States. Election season always invokes an excess of emotions as individuals absorb advertisements, stump speeches, and debates. It doesn't matter your political affiliation because once you cast your ballot you've voted against half the population. The popular vote margin of victory hovers around 50%, so half the country will love the result and the other half will hate it.

Investors are emotional about this election as well. They'll try to position their portfolio to benefit from the winner's platform. Some investors will want to sell their stocks and wait for the election parade to pass. The "sell all" investors will convert their portfolios to cash before the election and then buy into the market after it's over. These investors, along with a few million other traders, are trying to time the market before the results are in so they can avoid a drop in the market and then buy stocks once it's over. Sounds easy.

Does it make sense to try and time the market around the election? A recent report from Dimensional Fund Advisors found the election month generated about the same volatility as a typical month. A majority of the time the election year monthly market returns fell in a range of negative 2% to a positive 6%.[1] These ranges compare favorably to non-election years.

I echo the sentiments of Dimensional Fund Advisors as they recently wrote in their third quarter report, "Investors would be well-served to avoid the temptation to make significant changes to a long-term investment plan based upon these sorts of predictions."

In reviewing the past 10 elections, dating back to 1976, an investor who purchased stocks on November 1st of the year of the election (1976, 1980, and so on) generated an average annual return of 7.53%.[2] One who purchased stock during Calvin Coolidge's presidency in 1926 generated an average annual return of 10%. A $10,000 purchase in the Standard & Poor's 500 in 1926 was worth $53 million at the end of December 2015.[3]

Here are few election tips for your portfolio.

Focus on your long-term goals. The election will come and go, and investors will soon shift their focus to other fun topics like earnings, interest rates, and taxes.

Our government comprises three branches: Executive, Legislative, and Judicial. Our founding fathers realized the

---

[1] Dimensional Fund Advisors 2016 3rd Quarter Review.
[2] Morningstar Office Hypothetical Tool.
[3] Dimensional Fund Advisors 2016 Matrix Book.

beauty of checks and balances, and so should you. A well-diversified portfolio is a vote for investment success.

Invest early and invest often. The sooner you start investing the better your long-term results will be.

I'm Bill Parrott and I approve this message.

The business of America is business. ~ Calvin Coolidge

October 16, 2016

Dow Jones = 18,086.40

69   The Law of Large Numbers

How often do you think about numbers? I think about them all the time. On a recent drive from Houston to Austin, I started thinking about numbers, wondering how much money a college graduate will earn over her working lifetime. Per the National Association of Colleges and Employers, the average starting salary for a graduate last year was $50,219.[1] A graduate from the class of 2015 might work for 45 years. If she gets a 2% annual raise during her career, she'll earn over $3.6 million.

On the surface, $3.6 million appears to be a lot of money. But what does it mean for our recent graduate?

She joins a company with a 401(k) and contributes 10% of her pay to the plan. Over her life she'll contribute $360,000.

She buys a home for $250,000 with a 4%, 30-year mortgage. The interest and principal payments will cost her $343,440 over the life of her loan. This doesn't include taxes or insurance which will, of course, add to the cost.

She gets married and starts a family. She and her husband eventually have two kids. The couple will spend about

---

[1] http://www.naceweb.org/job-market/compensation/overall-starting-salary-for-class-of-2015-graduates-up-4-3-percent/.

$500,000 raising their children.² They'll spend another $760,000 for food.³

Sending their children to a public university will cost them another $600,000.⁴

During her 45-year working career this family of four might own 12 cars. Purchasing 12 cars with an average price of $30,000 and a typical 60-month loan will cost the family over $395,000.

She and her family like to travel and they'll spend more than $285,000 on trips.⁵

How about healthcare? This young family could spend over $715,000 on premiums over their working career.⁶

Let's recap the numbers:

---

²https://blogs.wsj.com/economics/2016/06/22/how-much-does-it-cost-to-raise-a-child/, Lum Thuy Vo, Wall Street Journal, June 22, 2016.

³ https://www.usatoday.com/story/news/nation/2013/05/01/grocery-costs-for-family/2104165/Nancy Hellmich, USA Today, May 1, 2013.

⁴ Money Guide Pro College Cost Calculator, 4 years at a public university.

⁵ https://www.vacationkids.com/Vacations-with-kids/bid/302770/How-Much-Does-A-Family-Vacation-Cost, Sally Black, July 12, 2013, Vacation Kids Website.

⁶ https://www.webmd.com/health-insurance/insurance-costs/insurance-cost-calculator, accessed October 20, 2016.

- Lifetime income = $3.6 million.
- Retirement plan contributions = $360,000
- Mortgage = $343,000
- Food = $760,000
- Education = $600,000
- Cars = $395,000
- Travel = $285,000
- Healthcare = $715,000

These expenses add up to $3.45 million, leaving little left over for other fun family items like taxes and home repairs.

What should our recent graduate do? It's important for her to live within her means. If she makes $2 and spends $1, then life will be good. She should also create a family budget to identify where her money is going. In addition, she should invest for the long term by owning stocks of all sizes and focus on creating generational wealth. Last, she should enjoy the journey!

All hard work brings a profit, but mere talk leads only to poverty. ~ Proverbs 14:23

October 21, 2016

Dow Jones = 18,145.71

70   Spooky Numbers

Americans will spend more than $2.5 billion on Halloween this year. Candy Corn, M&M's, Milky Way, and Junior Mints will be tossed around on Halloween night. In addition to candy, Americans will spend money on elaborate costumes, haunted houses, and extravagant decorations.

When I was a young trick-or-treater I'd bring home a king's ransom worth of candy. One lady on my street gave each masquerader five shiny pennies. Each year it was the same thing – five pennies. Today, the inflation adjusted value of her gift is 11 cents.

Here are a few more scary numbers.

Per Time Magazine, 1 in 3 Americans has $0.00 saved for retirement and 42% of millennials have yet to start saving for their golden years.[1]

Individuals in their 60s have an average retirement balance of $172,000.[2] If you withdraw 4%, you'll generate $6,880 in annual income.

The average monthly Social Security check is $1,176. How long can you support your current lifestyle on $1,176? Social

---

[1] http://time.com/money/4258451/retirement-savings-survey/ Elyssa Kirkham, March 14, 2016.
[2] https://www.fool.com/retirement/general/2016/03/21/the-average-american-has-this-much-saved-for-retir.aspx, Matthew Frankel, March 21, 2016, The Motley Fool.

Security accounts for 38% of a retiree's income.[3] Where does the other 62% come from? You!

A 25-year-old worker who is saving $10,000 annually until age 67 will have $2.3 million. If he waits until age 50 to get serious about saving for retirement, his $10,000 annual savings will be worth $308,402, a difference of almost $2 million.[4] Procrastination can be frightening when trying to plan for retirement.

What can you do to insure you have a sweet retirement?

Start saving early. The earlier you start saving for retirement, the more money you'll have in your bucket. On Halloween night if I left at 7:00 instead of 8:00, I'd got more candy.

If you work for a company with a retirement plan, sign up as soon as you're eligible. A worker under the age of 50 can contribute $18,000 while a worker over the age of 50 can save $24,000. If these amounts aren't in your budget, try to save at least 10% of your income.

---

[3] https://money.usnews.com/money/retirement/articles/2011/08/30/retirees-increasingly-depending-on-social-security, Emily Brandon, U.S. News, August 30, 2011.

[4] Money Guide Pro Cost of Waiting Calculator, growth rate of 7%, past performance is no guarantee of future results.

Automate your savings. Automation will allow you to make regular contributions to your investment accounts. You can automate everything – savings, IRAs, 401(k)s, etc.

Don't get spooked by stock market dips and dives. Stocks have fallen and risen for hundreds of years. When it does go through a few lean years, use it as an opportunity to buy quality companies. When I returned home from trick-or-treating I endured a few popcorn balls, apples, and pennies before I got to the good stuff. It's the same with investing – your patience will be rewarded.

Last, have a plan. Your financial plan will help guide you to the promised land. Before my friends and I left the house in pursuit of candy riches, we planned our route. We knew the houses with the best candy, so we planned accordingly!

The older you get, the harder it is to find someone willing to share a horse costume with you. ~ Anonymous

October 25, 2016

Dow Jones = 18,169.27

71 The Sun Will Come Up Tomorrow

The story of Little Orphan Annie has been entertaining the public since 1924. The comic strip first appeared as a political cartoon criticizing organized labor and the New Deal.[1] Annie and her trusted dog, Sandy, were looking for her parents before she finally gets adopted by Daddy Warbucks. She sings the famous song *Tomorrow* to focus on better days ahead and she believes tomorrow will always bring hope.

Our country needs a little sunshine and hope as we march to the polls on November 8th. As we move closer to Election Day investors are getting jittery. Stock market volatility is increasing as investors look to hedge or sell most of their portfolio until the hard knocks pass. Short term, headline thinking is ruling the day, but don't let it damage your long-term financial results.

When the sun rises on Wednesday we'll have a new President of the United States of America. What will you do? Will this election have any bearing on your financial future? Will your financial goals change? Will you adjust your spending? Will your expenses go away? Will your retirement date change?

A 30-year old investor might experience 17 Presidents during her lifetime. Does it make sense for her to adjust her portfolio with each election? Maybe. However, it's more important for

---

[1] https://en.wikipedia.org/wiki/Little_Orphan_Annie, accessed October 31, 2016.

her to focus on the things she can control, like spending and saving.

Here are a few investment thoughts as we hurtle towards the election.

Don't make any short-term, irrational, or emotional decisions because of what you read, see, or hear. Short-term thinking will sink your long-term goals. In a study by Morningstar, investors earned 2.49% less than the mutual funds they owned over a 10-year period because of emotional trading decisions![2]

Missing the 15 best trading days can also harm your returns. Per Dimensional Funds, an investor who adopted a buy and hold strategy from 1970 to 2015 averaged 10.27%. Missing the 15 best trading days dropped your average to 7.95% – a difference of 2.32% per year![3] The buy and hold investor investing $1,000 per year ended up with more than $780,000 while the investor who missed the 15 best trading days ended up with about $380,000. Our buy and hold investor ended up with $400,000 more than our little market timer.

---

[2] https://www.investopedia.com/articles/basics/10/how-to-avoid-emotional-investing.asp, Kristina Zucchi, CFA, Investopedia, September 27, 2016.

[3] Dimensional Fund Advisors, Reacting Can Hurt Performance – 1970 to 2015, accessed October 31, 2016.

Asset allocation and diversification can be your best investing friends during times of market duress. A portfolio of large, small, and international companies mixed with bonds and cash will reduce your risk. An investor whose portfolio consists of 100% stocks can reduce his risk by adding bonds. If he moved to an allocation of 60% stocks and 40% bonds, his risk exposure drops by over 38%.[4]

The election is going to come and go, and markets will go up and down. I don't know who is going to win or what the market will do but I know the sun will come up tomorrow!

I'm not giving up. Don't you give up! ~ Daddy Warbucks

October 29, 2016

Dow Jones = 18,142.42

---

[4] Morningstar Office, Portfolio Diversification and Performance presentation, accessed October 31, 2016.

72   Puzzle Pieces

During the holiday season, my family and I like to put together a puzzle or two. It has become a holiday tradition in our home. When my daughter was young the puzzles were simple and easy to manage. As she grew older they became more complex, with thousands of pieces. Each puzzle size has its pros and cons. Smaller puzzles were easy to assemble, but if we lost a piece or two it didn't look like much of a puzzle when finished. Larger puzzles take a few days to complete and it didn't matter if we lost a couple of pieces because we still had close to 1,000.

The Morningstar database currently tracks 109,000 global stocks. Can you imagine trying to put together a 100,000-piece puzzle?

When constructing your investment portfolio how do you pick the best stocks from the 109,000 publicly traded companies? Dividend? PE? Earnings? Price? Of course, the stocks you choose will depend on the amount of money you're going to invest.

Let's say your investment capital is $50,000 and you decide to invest $5,000 into each company. In this scenario, you'll be able to purchase 10 stocks. Of the 109,000 stocks in the Morningstar database, how do you choose the 10 best? The 10 companies you pick represent .0001% of the stocks in the database. And what do you know that Warren Buffett, Peter Lynch, or David Swensen don't know?

A View from the Perch

Let's up your investment capital to $500,000. You decide to keep your individual stock investment to $5,000 for diversification purposes. You now own 100 companies, so you should be able to achieve a balanced portfolio but how do you follow them? Do you have the time, interest, discipline, and emotion to keep tabs on your growing portfolio?

How about a $5 million portfolio? Even though your account has grown you still want to invest $5,000 into each company so you now own 1,000 stocks. If you own 1,000 stocks, it had better be your full-time job! As your account grows, so too will your position limits. In an account of this size, you'll probably want to invest between $100,000 to $200,000 into each company.

How many stocks do you need to own to achieve portfolio diversification? 10? 25? 100? 400? A study by the American Association of Individual Investors suggests a portfolio north of 400 stocks. Owning 400 stocks can reduce your diversifiable risk by 95%.[1] Dimensional Fund Advisors recommends owning 11,000 stocks to achieve diversification bliss.[2]

How can you achieve diversification? Here are two thoughts.

---

[1] http://www.aaii.com/journal/article/how-many-stocks-do-you-need-to-be-diversified-.touch, AAII Journal, Daniel J. Burnside, July 2004

[2] https://my.dimensional.com/insight/purely_academic/23691/, Effective Diversification and the Number of Stocks, Jim Davis, September 26, 2008.

Buy a lot of stocks. You can, of course, buy as many stocks as you want. I once worked with an advisor who would purchase one to two shares of a company. He owned a sliver of hundreds of stocks. I never understood his investment "strategy." Jim Cramer suggests owning between five and ten companies and committing an hour of research for each stock owned.[3] In his model, if you own 100 companies, you should commit 100 hours to research.

Purchase stock index mutual funds. Index funds will allow you to own thousands of companies. The advantage of owning index funds is that you can achieve diversification at a low cost. With a purchase of four, five, or ten index funds you can also simplify your financial life. It's much easier to follow a few funds as compared to tracking thousands of companies.

There are many roads to financial success, so travel on one that makes sense for you and your family. Your goal should be to grow your wealth, so you can support your family's lifestyle.

It's not about the pieces, it's how they fit together. ~ Anonymous

November 1, 2016

Dow Jones = 18,037.10

---

[3] http://www.cnbc.com/id/100765791, Stocks, How Many Is too Many? Lee Brodie, October 7, 2014.

73 Now What?

The election is over, and Mr. Trump has been elected the 45th President of the United States. Now what? For the past 18 months or so America has been polarized by the election. Investors were absorbed with political bantering and now they'll direct their gaze to the next hurdle, most likely a decision from the Federal Reserve on interest rates. Should investors always zero in on the near-term hurdle?

Edwin Moses is one of the most decorated athletes of our time. He made a career of jumping over hurdles. He won the Olympic Gold medal in the 1976 Montreal Games by winning the 400-meter hurdles in world record time. After the Olympics he dominated his sport by winning 122 consecutive races, a feat that landed him in the Guinness Book of Records.[1]

Mr. Moses had to clear 10 hurdles while running once around the track. I'm sure he didn't panic when he arrived at the first hurdle because he had a plan and he still had to clear nine more before he won his race. To be successful, a hurdler must look beyond the near hurdle and focus his eyes on the horizon. A runner with attention riveted to the closest hurdle probably didn't fare well in the race.

---

[1] http://edwinmoses.com/icon_bio.html, accessed November 7, 2016.

Unlike Mr. Moses, investors will always have hurdles. Is it wise to pay attention to these obstacles? The news media and industry "experts" want to divert your eyes from your goals and focus on the latest threat to your investment survival. Look beyond the near-term issue and focus on your long-term investment goals.

How can you be a great investor and avoid the hurdles?

Lock your eyes on the investment horizon and pay attention to your financial goals.

Diversify your investments across stocks, bonds, and cash.

Concentrate on things you can control like saving and spending.

Be greedy when others are fearful, as Warren Buffett wisely advised.

Establish a cash emergency fund so you're not forced to sell your long-term holdings at disastrous prices.

Avoid market timing. Trying to catch the top or bottom of a market cycle historically hasn't worked well for investors.

Don't trade excessively as this will increase your costs and fees. There is an inverse relationship between the fees you pay and the returns you generate.

Elections come and go. Markets go up and down. The sun rises and sets. If you focus on the long term, good things can happen.

***Obstacles are those frightening things you see when you take your eyes off your goal.* ~ Henry James.**

November 9, 2016

Dow Jones = 18,589.69

74   What's Up, Doc?

While growing up, I'd park myself in front of our family TV with a bowl of Fruit Loops and feast on a heavy dose of Looney Tunes. I needed my fill of Bugs Bunny, Foghorn Leghorn, Daffy Duck, and Yosemite Sam for my day to start off on the right foot.

Bugs Bunny is a smooth operator. He's calm, cool, and collected. The only time I remember him losing his temper was during the show *Rebel Rabbit*. In *Rebel Rabbit*, Bugs was upset that the bounty for a rabbit was only 2 cents, so he went on a rampage.[1] Despite this one episode he's wise beyond his ears.

In addition to Bugs Bunny, Tweety and Road Runner are composed and sensible. They'd make fantastic investors. They were under constant attack from Daffy Duck, Elmer Fudd, Yosemite Sam, Sylvester, or Wile E. Coyote. Regardless of these threats they thought rationally and never lost their composure and, as a result, they would always outsmart their foes.

On the other hand, Daffy Duck, Tasmania Devil, Yosemite Sam, and Wile E. Coyote were overly emotional. Their emotions would get the better of them and usually in a dramatic way. To give credit to Daffy, Yosemite, and Wile they appeared to start

---

[1] http://www.imdb.com/title/tt0041785/, Rebel Rabbit 1949, accessed November 13, 2016.

with a pretty good game plan. However, when the plan did not work they reacted with fits of rage and anger.

Sylvester and Foghorn Leghorn were overflowing with confidence and bravado. But they were a little too optimistic in their abilities. Foghorn Leghorn was probably the worst in his overconfidence as he was constantly outwitted by Barnyard Dawg and little Henerey Hawk.

What can we learn from these Looney Tunes?

To be a successful investor, think like Bugs, Tweety, and Road Runner. Their peaceful demeanor and silent confidence has treated them well. They don't get rattled by current events and continue to focus on the task at hand. It helps to remain calm despite external pressures when you invest. The recent presidential election is an excellent example of forces beyond our control. The screaming headline news, angry posts, and flurry of tweets caused much angst for investors. However, those who remained calm during the trials and tribulations were rewarded with higher stock prices.

An investor who, like Daffy Duck or Yosemite Sam, is overly emotional will have trouble creating long-term wealth. If emotions get the better of you, it would be wise to hire an advisor who can walk you through the valley during difficult markets. Emotions are usually tied to stock market gyrations, so one way to calm your nerves is to lower your exposure to stocks and diversify your holdings across different asset classes.

Having an overabundance of confidence is normally good. Too much, however, can be a bad thing when it comes to investing. Overconfidence may block your ability to remain flexible during times of market upheaval. It helps to be humble with the stock market and it's okay to admit when you're wrong and cut your losses. Sylvester and Foghorn Leghorn always had to be right, and consequently they were usually wrong.

It's been said that life imitates art and watching Looney Tunes cartoons proves it!

That's All Folks! ~ Porky Pig

November 17, 2016

Dow Jones = 18,903.82

75   Do You Have Preferred Status?

Who doesn't like preferred status? It's nice to be preferred when boarding an airplane, entering a movie theater, or getting a table in a crowded restaurant. Preferred status carries a certain level of prestige.

One investment that deserves the preferred moniker is the preferred stock.

Preferred stocks are interesting investments. They're usually issued at $25 per share and pay a quarterly dividend. The investments are non-callable for five years and then they can be redeemed by the issuing corporation. If the issue is not called after five years, it's possible your investment may have a maturity date of 20, 30, 40 years or more. You don't have to hold your investment for multiple decades because you can sell it at any time. If you decide to sell, you may get back more or less than your original investment. After the non-call date, a company can redeem your holding on any interest payment date.

With the recent rise in rates, many preferred stocks have traded down in value, giving new investors a nice entry point. The rate rise has pushed the price of these investments below their offer price of $25. Bank of America and Capital One currently have issues yielding over 6% while Wells Fargo, Southern California Edison, and J.P. Morgan have yields north of 5%. Several companies are paying 7%, 8%, 9%, or more.

Here's how a preferred stock works. A company issues shares at $25 per share with a 6% dividend. If you buy 1,000 shares at $25, your total cost will be $25,000. The 6% dividend generates $1,500 per year or $375 per quarter. For five years the company can't redeem your shares. At the end of the five-year term the company can call in your shares. If your shares are called, your $25,000 investment will be credited to your account. If they don't call your shares, you'll continue to receive $1,500 per year for as long as you own your shares. These investments trade on the stock exchanges so you can buy or sell them at any time.

What's the downside to owning these fixed income investments? I believe there are two risks. If rates rise, the value of your preferred stock will lose value. A highly rated preferred stock may trade to a price of $18 or $19 from their offer price of $25 per share if interest rates climb. The other risk is related to longevity. If your preferred stock isn't redeemed after five years, it may turn into a long-term holding. A company that issued a preferred stock in a low interest rate environment has little incentive to redeem your shares during a rising rate environment.

Preferred stocks are riskier than U.S. Treasuries, municipal or corporate bonds. However, a small allocation to your account can help you generate above-average income. How much should you invest in this category? I'd suggest an allocation of 5% to 15% of your fixed income portfolio.

As interest rates continue to bounce around it may pay to add preferred investments to your portfolio.

Probable impossibilities are to be preferred to improbable possibilities. ~ Aristotle

November 20, 2016

Dow Jones = 18,956.69

76   Are You an Above-Average Driver?

Several studies have shown that most people consider themselves to be above-average drivers. In some studies, the percentage of people who think they are above average is as high as 93%, a mathematical impossibility.[1] You've seen the driver darting in and out of traffic trying to find the fastest lane only to catch up to him a few miles down the road stuck behind a slow-moving 18-wheeler. As you pass Speed Racer you smirk because you know the law of averages are in your favor when driving on a crowded highway.

With the recent rout in the bond market I've talked to several investors questioning the wisdom of owning a bond fund, a slow-moving vehicle. They want to move their money to the hot sector. They're not alone. Individuals have been selling bond funds by the billions and buying hot sector funds. I remind them about the value of diversification and how over the long term it will be their best friend. Trying to find the fastest moving sector is like racing toward the fast lane on a freeway. It's important to own a diversified portfolio so you can take advantage of all sectors and markets.

Is there a better way for you to take advantage of this investor traffic jam? Can you find a highway with nothing but open

---

[1] http://washingtonsblog.com/2015/05/illusory-superiority-related-psychological-phenomena-and-the-importance-of-cross-cultural-exposure.html, Robert Barsocchini, May 1, 2015.

road in front of you? Can you lower your stress level by discovering the road less travelled? Yes.

Here are three diversified Dimensional mutual funds that can help drive your portfolio:

- Dimensional U.S. Large Cap Value Fund (DFLVX)
- Dimensional U.S. Small Cap Fund (DFSTX)
- Dimensional International Value Fund (DFIVX)

An equally weighted investment in these three delivered an average annual return of 9.15% for the past 22 years. A $30,000 investment in this three-fund portfolio in 1994 would have grown to $206,000 on October 31, 2016.[2]

How about the hot sector? If you only owned these three funds, would you have been driving on the wrong side of the road? Would you have missed the best sectors? No. These three funds own more than 2,800 securities covering every investment sector and category.

Two of the sectors currently generating the most attention because of the election results are financials and infrastructure. These funds currently have 22.5% of their holdings invested in financial companies to give you exposure to 630 companies. The allocation to industrials is 13.75%, which means you own 385 stocks in this sector.

---

[2] Morningstar Office Hypothetical Tool.

It would be awesome to always travel in the fast lane, but it's not possible. Besides it causes a lot of stress and road rage. The same is true with investing. Trying to always find the fastest stock or sector is extremely challenging and taxing. Your road to financial harmony may be lined with a few low-cost mutual funds.

Americans will put up with anything provided it doesn't block traffic. ~ Dan Rather

November 28, 2016

Dow Jones = 19,097.90

77   15,902 Stock Picks for 2017

Tis the season for Wall Street and financial magazines to identify their best stock picks for 2017. In a few weeks we'll start to see publications, websites, and blog posts highlight their best selections for the coming year. I want to add my name to the list of people making bold stock selections for 2017, so I've selected 15,902 companies. I'm hopeful a few of these companies will turn out to be big winners.

What was my screening process? How did I select these top stocks? I selected six diversified mutual funds from Dimensional Fund Advisors. These funds own 15,902 companies. Here are the six funds: DFA Core Equity – DFEOX, DFA Micro Cap – DFSCX, DFA Small Cap – DFSTX, DFA Real Estate – DFREX, DFA International Core – DFIEX, and DFA Emerging Markets – DFCEX.[1]

An equally weighted portfolio of these funds, rebalanced annually, generated the following returns.

One-year return of 8.9%. A $60,000 investment one year ago is now worth $65,300.

Three-year average annual return of 5.4%. A $60,000 investment three years ago is now worth $70,300.

Five-year average annual turn of 11.2%. A $60,000 investment five years ago is now worth $102,500.

---

[1] Morningstar Office Hypothetical Tool.

10-year average annual return of 5.9%. A $60,000 investment 10 years ago is now worth $106,000.

In addition to getting access to thousands of companies, your low-cost portfolio covers the world, with 75% of your holdings in the United States, and 25% international.

Rather than picking the best five or six stocks for 2017 focus your energy on identifying your top five or six financial goals. Is this your year to open an IRA or reduce debt? How about creating an emergency fund or establishing a budget? Buying a second home or funding an education account? The benefits of spending time getting your financial house in order will serve you better than buying five or six hot stocks.

Another suggestion is to increase your financial knowledge so you can become a more informed investor. Here are a few investment classics you can add to your Christmas list.

- *The Only Investment Guide You'll Ever Need* – Andrew Tobias
- *Bogle on Mutual Funds* – John C. Bogle
- *Beating the Street* – Peter Lynch
- *A Random Walk Down Wall Street* – Burton G. Malkiel
- *Where are the Customers' Yachts?* – Fred Schwed, Jr.
- *The Most Important Thing Illuminated* – Howard Marks

- *Stocks for the Long Run* – Jeremy J. Siegel

As we roll into the new year keep your eyes focused on the long term. Asset allocation, diversification, and low fees win in the end.

Well, I think the secret is if you have a lot of stocks, some will do mediocre, some will do okay, and if one or two of 'em go up big time, you produce a fabulous result. And I think that's the promise to some people. ~ Peter Lynch

December 2, 2016

Dow Jones = 19,170.42

78   It Will Rain on May 23rd, 2025. At Noon

Will it rain on May 23rd, 2025? I have no idea. It may. Who knows. If it does, I'll look smart. I have a 50/50 chance. It either will rain or it won't. A major-league baseball player who hits safely 50% of the time and ends up with a batting average of .500 would be considered the greatest athlete of all time. An NFL place kicker who makes 50% of his field goal attempts gets fired.

Investors and media folk put their faith in stock analyst and treat their picks and price targets as Gospel even though they're only right about 50% of the time. In a 2012 report from Nerd Wallet they found that analysts who followed the 30 stocks in the Dow Jones Industrial Average were right in their stock picks 51% of their time.[1] In a deeper study from researchers at the University of Waterloo and Boston College, they found analysts missed their price targets about 70% of the time.[2] Regardless, analysts continue to make bold stock

---

[1] https://www.nerdwallet.com/blog/investing/investing-data/investment-stock-analyst-ratings-stockpicking-research-wrong/, Nerd Wallet, April 16, 2013.

[2] http://business.financialpost.com/investing/analysts-target-prices-rarely-accurate-global-study-finds, David Pett, March 7, 2013.

predictions and investors hang their hat on these recommendations.

One way to beat the analysts and Wall Street at their own game is to own a basket of index funds. With an index portfolio, you don't have to worry about stock picks or price targets because you'll have the opportunity to own companies from all over the world.

In a recent *Wall Street Journal* article about market predictions, analysts have prophesied about positive market returns every year since 2000 even though the stock market has fallen about a third of the time. The 2008 forecast from Wall Street strategists were pointing towards a positive year. In 2009, their outlook was dire.[3]

Can you succeed without Wall Street? I believe you can with a simple strategy of owning a diversified basket of low cost index funds.

The following portfolio generated an average annual return of 8.25% over the past 12 years. This year, through November, it's up 9.95%. Here's the all-equity portfolio:[4]

- IVV – iShares S&P 500 Index
- VO – Vanguard Mid-Cap Index
- IJR – iShares S&P 600 Index

---

[3] Wall Street Journal, James Mackintosh, December 9, 2016.
[4] Morningstar Hypothetical Tool. November 2011 to November 2016.

- VNQ – Vanguard Real Estate Index
- EFA – iShares MSCI EAFE International Index
- EEM – iShares MSCE Emerging Markets Index

During its 12-year run, it had three losing years; the worst occurred in 2008 when it lost 40.8%. It did rebound a year later with a gain of 38.8% followed by a 19.4% jump in 2010.

As we move toward 2017 it may be time for you to adjust your New Year's resolutions and focus on a low-cost, diversified, index portfolio. My prediction is that you'll find it beneficial towards achieving your long financial goals.

Never make predictions, especially about the future.* ~ *Casey Stengel

December 9, 2016

Dow Jones = 19,756.85

79   The Usual Suspects

The Usual Suspects is one of the most creative films ever made. Verbal, the main character, narrates the story as he sits in the detective's office detailing the horrors of Kaiser Soze. We're gripped with suspense as we try to figure out who he is. The movie is full of twists and turns and at the end we realize Verbal has been fabricating his story. As he walks down the street we see him transform before our eyes and we're left wondering if he's Kaiser Soze. As the detective looks around his office he realizes he may have had him the entire time. Are Verbal and Kaiser Soze one and the same? We may never know because we see what we want to see.

Today we're trying to figure out what Trump's Presidency means for our economy as one of the key components of his campaign is to fix our nation's infrastructure. Initial price projections for these projects are $1 trillion. As one who's crisscrossed the country by planes, trains, and automobiles, I'm all for improving our nation's public transportation system.

Interest rates have soared since the election as investors anticipate mounting inflation due to increases in government spending. As a result, investors have sold bonds by the billions. The yield on the 10-year U.S. Treasury has risen from 1.37% to 2.6%, a rise of 89% since Mr. Trump was elected. At this pace, the yield will be 4.9% by his inauguration and 33% by the end of his first 100 days in office. Of course, this rate of change can't last. Regardless, investors have been selling bonds and buying stocks at a furious rate.

A View from the Perch

We've seen this movie before as investors sell one asset class en masse to buy another. It happened in January of this year when individuals sold billions of dollars' worth of stock funds to buy bond funds. What happened next? The stock market climbed dramatically, leaving bond holders disappointed.

Will building and spending start on day one of his presidency? Are projects shovel ready? I doubt it. It will take years before we see completion of these projects. If you need proof, look no further than the Big Dig in Boston. It was one of our country's largest infrastructure projects. It started during Reagan's administration in 1982 and wasn't completed until 2007. If a new project starts today and follows the same path as the Big Dig, we'll have six more presidential elections before the projects are completed, so don't be in such a rush to make major portfolio changes.

What to make of these observations? Here are a few thoughts.

- Don't be in a hurry to sell your bond holdings. They complete the asset allocation pie and will play a big part in preserving your household wealth. Bonds will provide safety and income.
- If you're concerned interest rates will rise, park your money in a money market fund.
- Invest in a short-term bond ladder with U.S. Treasury Bills and Certificates of Deposits. You can create a ladder with investments coming due every three months. It will give you liquidity

and the ability to pounce on higher rates if they come.
- January is a perfect time to rebalance your investments. Rebalancing will help reduce risk. For example, if you started the year with 50% stocks and 50% bonds by the end of the year your mix may be 70% stocks and 30% bonds. Your risk exposure has risen above your original allocation. In this example, you sell 20% of your stocks and buy 20% more bonds to realign your portfolio back to your original allocation.
- Align your investments to your goals. Buying a second home, paying for college, or funding retirement will have different time horizons so make sure your investments are linked accordingly. Invest in bonds for short-term goals and stocks for long-term ones.
- Follow your financial plan. It will give you the necessary clues for a successful investment future.

Verbal had a plan and it appeared to work well. His strategy allowed him to live another day. Your plan will allow you to survive several market conditions.

There is nothing more deceptive than an obvious fact. ~ Arthur Conan Doyle

A View from the Perch

December 18, 2016

Dow Jones = 19,883.06

80 Extra! Extra! Read All About It!

I love watching old movies when there's a young kid shouting at passersby to get a copy of the local paper. The young entrepreneur is standing on a busy street corner with stacks of newspapers highlighting the most important news printed above the fold. Hey mister, "Did you hear about…"

In the old days it took time for news to travel around the globe. Pre-Internet, our news moved by radio, TV, and newspaper. Today, it's instantaneous and delivered through billions of personal and professional outlets broadcasted in real time regardless of its origin.

Headline risk can move a market up or down, sometimes violently. It can upset the entire market or just a single company.

A new wrinkle to headline risk is fake news. It's on the rise and has a higher probability of going viral as compared to real news.[1]

How should you approach headline risk? Here are a few suggestions:

- If you own a stock getting thumped by a news story, check the source. Look to sites you trust to

---

[1] https://www.vox.com/2016/11/16/13626318/viral-fake-news-on-facebook, Aja Romano, November 16, 2016.

verify if the news is true. If it's true, reevaluate the reasons why you bought the stock. Should you buy or sell based on the facts? Is the news material and will it have a permanent impact on your investment?
- Don't react. Wait for it to run its course and the volatility to pass. Most investors overreact to news stories and it's possible your investment will recover from the sell-off.
- If the entire market is being dragged down, use it as an opportunity to add to your stock holdings. Headline risk is usually short lived.

As the world becomes smaller and more connected, take a moment to disconnect. You should buy stocks for the long haul, so don't get carried away by short term headlines.

An honest witness does not deceive, but a false witness pours out lies. ~ Proverbs 14:5

December 20, 2016

Dow Jones = 19,974.62

81   12c Things I Learned from My Calculator

In a world of chats, posts, opinions, and rhetoric it's nice to have a trusted advisor who can perform without emotion or fear. My advisor tells me what I need to hear, not what I want to. I get the facts and only the facts. My trusted source is available 24/7. What's this magical source of information? It's my Hewlett Packard 12c calculator, an RPN juggernaut. While I watch the news, my reliable partner keeps me grounded and helps me separate wheat from chaff. My little HP12c has been with me through rising and falling markets, rate hikes, and rate cuts.

Here are 12 things I've learned in my years crunching numbers on the 12c:

1. If I save $1,000 per month for 30 years at 10%, I'll have a nest egg worth $2.26 million! The best opportunity to generate the long-term return in the market is to buy consistently and hold on to your investment regardless of if the market is rising or falling.

2. If I procrastinate, I'll have less money. If I save $1,000 per month for 15 years at 10%, I'll end up with $414,000, a difference of $1.84 million!

3. The 12c helps me factor inflation into my original calculation. A 3% inflation rate will reduce my $2.6 million to $1.1 million.

4. If I invest in long-term government bonds, I'll end up with less money than if I invest in stocks. The historical return for bonds has been 5.6%. A monthly investment of $1,000 for 30-years will be worth $930,000.

5. When I add a 3% inflation rate to my historical bond return, the value drops to $537,000 after 30 years.

6. It helps me calculate the percentage gain or loss on bonds. A 30-year bond paying 3% will gain 22% if interest rates drop by 1%. If interest rates rise by 1%, I'll lose 17%.

7. The 12c tells me that if I want to reduce my exposure to bond losses I should buy a five-year bond. A five-year bond will lose 4.5% if interest rates rise by 1%. If I'm concerned about rising interest rates, I'll need to shorten my bond maturity dates. Of course, a five-year bond will also gain less if interest rates should fall. A 1% rate drop on a five-year bond will gain 4.7%.

8. It helps me keep my debts in check. My total monthly debt payments should be less than 38% of my gross income. If I make $10,000 per month, my total debt payments should be less than $3,800.

9. The 12c helps me calculate a mortgage payment to see if I can qualify for the home of my dreams. A home purchase of $500,000 with a 20% down payment and 4% interest rate means my monthly mortgage payment will be $1,909.

10. It will calculate my mortgage payoff date as well. If I add an extra $500 per month to my mortgage payment, my payoff

date will be 20 years rather than 30. This ten-year reduction will save me over $100,000 in interest.

11. The average new car purchase is $33,560. A five-year loan with a rate of 4.3% means a monthly payment of $622.

12. My calculator keeps my budget in line. I can calculate all my payments on my trusted device, helping me make better financial decisions.

My 12c reminds me that if I save money and keep my expenses low, good things can happen.

A businessman is a hybrid of a dancer and a calculator. ~ Paul Valery

December 26, 2016

Dow Jones = 19,945.04

82   Everybody Loves a Parade!

The 128th Rose Parade will ring in the new year. It's a rite of passage for many. I grew up watching it on TV and in person. My friends and I would arrive at the parade route around 4:00 in the afternoon on New Year's Eve to get front-row seats and then spend the next 12 to 16 hours enjoying the craziness on Colorado Boulevard.

It wasn't until years later that I realized that the Rose Parade doesn't just happen. It never occurred to me as a young visitor that people plan the parade. It takes years for a parade to come together. Themes are chosen, bands are picked, and duties assigned years in advance. I'm sure someone on the Tournament of Roses Parade Committee is already planning the 2018 Rose Parade.

Life is like a parade. It has a beginning and an end, with a whole lot of stuff happening in between. In life, you're the grand marshal, drum major, equestrian, float builder, float driver, and so on. You get to create your own parade. How can you design your perfect parade?

As we march toward the new year here are a few ideas for your successful route.

Plan. All successful parades start with a plan. It's what separates a successful parade from a poor one. In January you'll have the opportunity to start fresh, out with the old and in with the new. Will this be the year you complete your financial plan?

Help. The parade doesn't run itself. The Tournament of Roses has 31 committees planning and executing countless activities. They'll contribute more than 80,000 hours of their time for this year's parade.[1] Can you use some help with your investments? Planning? Taxes?

Diversify. Bands, floats, and horses make for an entertaining parade. Diversification within the parade is what makes it enjoyable because it has something for everyone. Your investment portfolio should be diversified as well. Diversification will allow you to participate in all types of markets.

Time. The parade covers five and a half miles as it makes its way down Colorado Boulevard. The pace and length of the parade allows spectators to get a long look at the participants. Your investment horizon should take time as well. A patient, long term investor will be rewarded.

Vision. The first Rose Parade was held in 1890. Its founders possessed a vision which has thrilled millions worldwide, benefiting generations of parade goers. Will your investment portfolio benefit generations?

I almost forgot. In addition to the parade there's also a football game.

Happy New Year!

---

[1] https://www.tournamentofroses.com/rose-parade, accessed December 29, 2016.

A rose by any other name would smell as sweet.* ~ *Shakespeare

December 19, 2016

Dow Jones = 19,819.78

83 Sticks and Stones

Sticks and stones may break my bones, but words will never hurt me. How many times have you heard that phrase on the playground? You've no doubt seen the scene before as two young kids stand nose to nose with hands on hips shouting at each other when one of the young combatants yells out sticks and stones. Of course, words do matter.

"Reckless words pierce like a sword, but the tongue of the wise brings healing." ~ Proverbs 12:18

The tongue of choice today is Twitter. 140 characters pierce like a sword in the arena of social media. It's fast and unfiltered, giving equal access to all users. However, some users have a larger pulpit than others. One of the largest pulpits now belongs to our President Elect, whose tweets are becoming infamous.

The Trump Twitter Trade, or T3, is in full force. A tweet from Trump can send your stock or industry down, as we've seen from Lockheed Martin, Toyota, and the biotech sector. The Trump Tweet is now a risk that investors must factor into their investment models.

What should you do if your stock is the subject of a Trump Twitter attack? Can you profit from a Trump Twitter Trade (T3)? Here a are few suggestions.

After the tweet has harpooned your stock, take a few moments to calculate the damage. Will it be long term or cause a permanent loss of capital? The odds are the tweet and the stock drop will be short lived. A sharp drop in your stock can be used as a buying opportunity – especially if you're a long-term investor.

Will the Trump tweet cause collateral damage? An assault on the biotech sector might bring down other sectors such as big pharma or hospital stocks. Can you find a diamond in the rough? Is it possible to profit from a stock that has no direct connection to the tweet?

If you're a trader, keep some extra cash on hand to take advantage of a Trump Twitter Trade. It might give you a buying opportunity for a stock or sector you've had your eye on for some time.

Index funds will help cushion the blow of a Twitter tirade. An index fund will own hundreds, if not thousands of stocks. A strike on one stock or sector may drive down the price of the index fund for a short time, giving you an opportunity to buy more.

A sector ETF or specialty index fund should be limited to 3% to 5% of your overall portfolio. A small weighting in your holdings will help reduce the impact of a Trump tweet.

A diversified portfolio of large, small, and international companies will also help cushion the blow. Your account should also include bonds and cash. A well-rounded and balanced portfolio will make you immune from a 140-character offensive.

As you construct your portfolio, focus on your long-term goals and financial plans. They'll be more beneficial to you than damage inflicted by a short-term tweet.

...but no man can tame the tongue. ~ James 3:8

January 15, 2017

Dow Jones = 19,826.76

84 Wax on. Wax off.

The Karate Kid appeared on the big screen in 1984. Daniel and his family moved from New Jersey to the shores of California, a surfer's paradise, and had a rough time acclimating to the culture. Mr. Miyagi rescued him and began teaching him to defend himself. He's a wise teacher who taught Daniel many life lessons. One such lesson was taught in the famous scene of "wax on, wax off." I grew up in Southern California, where waxing a car is a rite of passage. A good wax job takes time and is taxing, especially on a large car. It's a two-part job: wax on, wax off. This lesson, along with many more, helped Daniel learn to defend himself.

The stock market has its own version of "wax on, wax off." It's "risk on, risk off." When the market is climbing, the "risk on" trade is in force. When it's falling, the "risk off" trade is popular.

How do you know if it's a "risk on" or "risk off" market? Unfortunately, you can know only in hindsight. That's when you realize a "risk on" trade should've been applied to a rising market and a "risk off" trade would've been better in a falling market. The "risk on, risk off" trade isn't a predictive indicator.

In a "risk on" trade, you'll want to own stocks that are more volatile. How can you tell if one stock is more volatile than another? One indicator is the stock's beta, which is a measure of volatility. A beta more than 1 indicates it's more volatile than the stock market. For example, a stock with a beta of 1.2

should move 20% more than the market. If the stock market is up 10%, your stock should be up 12%.

Another indicator is the relative strength index, or RSI. A high RSI will indicate momentum in your stock and an RSI above 60 to 65 will indicate solid momentum. When RSI goes above 70 it may indicate that your stock is overbought. A stock with a high beta and strong RSI will treat you well in a risk on trade.

Of course, the party always ends, and then the "risk off" trade is in vogue. The best way to profit from a "risk off" trade is to sell your stocks and move your money to cash or U.S. Treasury investments. Cash and Treasuries won't lose value in the short term, especially during a market meltdown. The more adventurous trader can short stocks or purchase put options.[1] These high-risk strategies will often yield a profit in a falling market.

Trying to time the stock market and apply "risk on, risk off" is a risky proposition. A better strategy for most investors is to implement the "balance on" trade. With a "balance on" trade, you own a portfolio of stocks, bonds, and cash. A diversified portfolio will serve you better in the long run!

---

[1] Options involve risk and are not suitable for all investors. Short selling is an aggressive investment strategy and is not suitable for all investors.

Lesson not just karate only. Lesson for whole life. Whole life have a balance. Everything be better. ~ Mr. Miyagi

January 16, 2016

Dow Jones = 19,826.76

85   Are You a Control Freak?

Do you like to be in control? Need specifics? Have a hard time with delegation? Do you always have to be right? I'm not a control freak, but I like to have a say in the outcome. I prefer driving to flying because I feel like I'm in control even though I know flying is safer. When I board an airplane, I surrender control to the pilot and the laws of physics. She's well trained and the plane is well built, but I'm not in the cockpit, which makes me a tad nervous.

Investors try to control their stock purchases by doing their homework and research on companies. Investors feel entitled to have their stock rise because they have spent hours crunching numbers and doing their homework.

A few years ago, a neighbor's son purchased a few shares in a company whose store he frequented. After his purchase the earnings report was announced, and the stock dropped. He was upset because he had done his homework and the store he frequented was always crowded. A stock doesn't know if you own it and couldn't care less how much research you did prior to your purchase.

Investors also try to control the market through timing. Shareholders will move money in and out of stocks, trying to find the optimal time to buy or sell. This is a waste of time. The S&P 500 returned 9.2% from 1994 to 2013. An investor who missed the 50 best days during this run ended up with a return of -2.8%.[1]

What can you control? How much you spend and save. The more you save and the less you spend will mean more money in your pocket.

To make money in the stock market you need to control your emotions both on the upside and downside. When they rise, don't get overly excited. When they drop, don't get overly depressed. The stock market has been fluctuating longer than we've been alive.

Is it possible for you to change your mindset when stocks fall? Investors are more concerned about the market dropping than rising. Loss aversion is the definition given to people who are more concerned about avoiding losses than they are in generating gains. Can you change your cues or triggers during a market correction? If you're loss averse, stop focusing so much on the potential loss and start emphasizing the positive to find stocks or funds to purchase.

The best way to get rich in the stock market and create generational wealth is to buy when everybody else is selling. When the market is going down, investors tend to sell quality companies at discounted prices, giving you the opportunity to add to your holdings at attractive prices.

---

[1] https://www.fa-mag.com/news/the-difficulty-and-costs-of-timing-the-market-22128.html, Chris Meyer, June 15, 2015.

It takes time to change the mindset. You must give up some control and let the long-term forces of the stock market take over.

Let it go! ~ Elsa

January 17, 2017

Dow Jones = 19,826.76

86   Windsocks

An airport is a sophisticated operation relying on the latest and best technology. An airplane is an engineering marvel designed to travel among the stars and heavens. Technology used in the airline industry is advancing at the speed of a Boeing 787 with radar and instrument panels beyond recognition to the early pioneers of flight.

During my investment career, I've had the opportunity to work with several commercial airline pilots. They've circled the globe, flying all types of aircraft from the 747 to the Dreamliner. A former client was one of the original 747 pilots. He passed away last year, and I miss talking to him about his flying. We often discussed the technological advances as they emerged over the years.

This past Sunday, while waiting for my San Diego to Houston flight to take off, a bright orange windsock caught my attention. I thought it was ironic that we still rely on a $50 windsock to determine the wind's direction and speed.

The windsock is a simple, but needed, instrument for pilots and airports because it helps air traffic controllers guide pilots to the safest runway.

Investors depend on technology to help with investment decisions. Investment technology is increasing at a rapid rate and is used by all types of investors, from robo-advisors to high frequency traders. The level of sophistication it brings to investment firms, advisors, and clients is unparalleled. And these advances continue to propel the industry higher.

With all the technology available today, do investors need a windsock? I believe they do.

Windsock One: Planning. A pilot must file a flight plan to fly from San Diego to Houston and all points in between. She also uses a checklist before she taxis the plane to the runway. The flight plan and the checklist are essential for a successful flight. A financial plan will help you navigate a path to financial freedom. Your plan is unique to you and can deliver you to your desired destination.

Windsock Two: Index Funds. Index funds may be the ultimate windsock. They may be simple in structure, but they've helped investors access markets around the world. The index revolution continues to gain loft as investors pour billions of dollars into index funds.

Windsock Three: Diversification. An investor who diversifies her holdings will avoid long-term turbulence in her portfolio. Owning different types of investments will keep her portfolio aloft for a long time.

Windsock Four: Asset Allocation. Asset allocation and diversification often fly in the same formation and may even share a hanger or two. Asset allocation spreads your assets across stocks, bonds, and cash. Allocating your assets to different types of stocks and bonds will help your account avoid a hard landing. By investing your assets in large, small, and international holdings your account will benefit from domestic and global growth.

Windsock Five. Fees. The lower your investment fees, the less drag on your portfolio. Do you like to pay high fees? By controlling your costs, you'll be able to keep more money in your pocket.

As we continue to depend on technology, do yourself a favor and keep your eye on your investment windsocks. It will be beneficial to your investment success. As a note, I'm not a pilot but I'm an excellent passenger!

Happy flying!

They shall mount up with wings as eagles. ~ Isaiah 40:31

Dow Jones = 20,052.41

February 6, 2017

87 Dump the Trump Bump?

The stock markets (all of them) continue to soar to new heights. Since the presidential election, the Dow Jones Industrial Average is up 14.5%. Several experts are calling for the market to give back these gains and then some. One advisor has called for the stock market to fall as far as 11,500, a drop of 44% from the current level.[1] Another has called for a "$68 trillion biblical collapse."[2] Finally, one economist has said the stock market is currently 80% overvalued.[3] Scary.

Is it wise to sell your stocks and depend on cash to ride out a market decline?

Let's look at some history.

The Standard & Poor's 500 Index is up 20% on a year over year basis. For the past five years it's up 93.3%. During the last 15 years it has gained 173.2%. Over the past 20 years it has risen 321%.

Looking back to 1987, an equal weighted portfolio owning the Vanguard S&P 500 Index Fund and the Vanguard Total Bond Fund generated a total return of 977%. A $100,000 investment is now worth $1,075,000. During the past 30 years, this portfolio's best year was in 1995 when it gained 27.80%. 2008

---

[1] https://www.cnbc.com/2016/06/22/dow-11500-is-a-matter-of-when-not-if-advisor.html, Michelle Fox, June 22, 2016.
[2] http://thesovereigninvestor.com/exclusives, JL Yastine, January 30, 2017.
[3] Ibid.

was the worst year as it dropped 16.57%. In this simple portfolio, you owned some of the market's best performers, including Apple, Microsoft, Amazon, Berkshire Hathaway, and Facebook.

What should you do as the market continues to climb to new heights? Here are a few suggestions.

Nothing. You don't have to do anything. History tells us that time in the stock market is the best way to create a mountain of money and produce generational wealth.

Diversify. If 100% of your money is invested in large companies, move some of it to other investments, like small or international companies.

Plan. What does your financial plan say? Have you arrived at your financial destination because of the markets rise? If so, sell some of your equity holdings and buy bonds to reduce your risk exposure.

Buy. If the market does drop 20% or 30%, buy the dip. Adding to your equity holdings when the market drops has proven to be a prudent financial strategy.

Give. If you have benefited from the rise in the market, take some gains and donate the money to your favorite cause or charity.

Of course, no one knows what the stock market will do, so the best strategy is to focus on your goals, save your money, and think long term.

Predicting rain doesn't count. Building arks does.* ~ *Warren Buffett

February 14, 2017

Dow Jones = 20,504.41

88   The Watchman

Four trillion is a massive number. Vanguard recently surpassed $4 trillion in client assets. By comparison, the market cap of Apple is $710 billion. Vanguard was founded in 1975 during the oil embargo recession and grew by putting the interests of their clients first, a novel concept on Wall Street in the mid-70s.

Vanguard is named after the 18th-century battleship HMS Vanguard, which means "in the forefront." It was led by the legendary investor John Bogle, who was in the forefront of the index revolution, having started one of the industry's first index funds. His idea wasn't well received, and the fund got off to a slow start. But today it's one of the largest mutual funds in the industry.[1]

A watchman is one who stands guard to protect others. He should be faithful, trustworthy, and put the interests of others first. How can you find your own watchman to help with your finances? Here are few suggestions.

Work with an advisor who is a fiduciary. By law a fiduciary must put your interest first. He must act in your best interest and disclose any conflicts of interest.

---

[1] https://about.vanguard.com/who-we-are/a-remarkable-history/, Vanguard Website, accessed February 15, 2017.

Work with a Certified Financial Planner®. An advisor who holds the CFP designation must go through years of study and pass a rigorous two-day exam. He must also undergo continuing education.

Work with an advisor who has a simple fee schedule. It should be easy to comprehend and doesn't break your bank.

Work with an advisor who has a servant's heart and returns your phone calls and emails in a timely fashion.

Work with an advisor who owns the investments he recommends to you and others.

Work with an advisor who shares similar values to your own.

Work with an advisor you can trust.

A hero is an ordinary individual who finds the strength to persevere and endure in spite of overwhelming obstacles. ~ Christopher Reeve

February 15, 2017

Dow Jones = 20,611.85

89   Active vs. Passive vs. You

The battle between active versus passive investment management rages on. The passive investment model is winning as billions of dollars pour into firms like Vanguard and Dimensional Fund Advisors. It makes sense, as the passive model outperforms the active one most of the time. In one study, 71% of active large cap money managers failed to beat the Standard & Poor's 500 Index.[1] In another study by Morningstar, only 4.5% of mid-cap money managers beat their corresponding benchmark.[2] It appears the choice is obvious.

However, the real battle isn't between active and passive. The real battle is active *and* passive against you! The real enemy to long-term financial success is the individual investor. Let's look at some famous investors and firms to make this point. Vanguard recently crossed $4 trillion in assets by offering low-cost index funds. Warren Buffet made billions by purchasing undervalued companies and holding them forever. Jim Chanos has made billions by shorting stocks of overvalued companies. John Tudor Jones made billions by actively trading currencies and commodities while Bill Gross made his billions by investing in bonds. These billionaires made their money with different

---

[1] https://www.investopedia.com/articles/investing/091015/lipper-rating-system-explained.asp, Sean Ross, September 10, 2015.

[2] http://hkbeta.morningstar.com/ods_images/2015Jun_Morningstar%20Active-Passive%20Barometer.pdf, Morningstar Active/Passive Barometer, June 2015, accessed February 20, 2017.

investment models. Through the years these highly successful investors honed their skills by focusing on what they do best. They stayed focused on their investment strategy and didn't abandon their belief system.

The same is true in sports. Bill Belichick, Geno Auriemma, and Nick Saban are geniuses at coaching their respective sports. These coaching legends didn't try to succeed at other sports or abandon their coaching philosophy when times were tough.

When markets are at extreme levels, individuals lose focus and abandon their investment strategies. When the market is rising sharply, investors want to chase the hot sector and sell investments not performing as well as others. In a rising market, bonds become less attractive. Who wants to own bonds with the stock market hitting all-time highs? This strategy works well until it doesn't. As markets fall, investors sell stocks and buy bonds. This popular pattern is known as buy high and sell low.

How can you invest like a billionaire?

Find an investment style that fits your personality.

Invest your time creating a financial plan.

Invest in simple models. If you understand what you own, you're more likely to stay invested through rising and falling markets.

Do not chase returns.

A View from the Perch

Do not panic when the market is falling.

Diversify your holdings.

Rebalance and review your strategy annually.

Save your money and keep your expenses low.

Think generationally.

As the market continues to march on, focus on your financial goals and don't get caught up chasing returns. A well-constructed investment plan and portfolio will treat you well for a long time.

The investor's chief problem, and even his worst enemy, is likely to be himself. ~ Benjamin Graham

February 20, 2017

Dow Jones = 20,743

90   My Dog's Life

On most mornings I run with my dog Cricket. She's a five-year-old yellow lab who loves running. Our morning ritual starts when I finish reading my daily dose of financial publications. When I remove my glasses and shut my iPad case she knows it's time to hit the streets. With her leash in my hand she starts to get excessively excited and run around in circles. Once the front door is ajar she shoots into the yard like a bottle rocket. I let her run off leash for a while, so she can burn off some excess energy.

A short while later we're reunited, and I attach her leash and settle into our run. Cricket knows where all the dogs on our route live and occasionally tries to veer off course to say hello. In addition to neighborhood dogs there is a multitude of distractions like squirrels, birds, or cats. Cricket will give them a slight nod and then continue on her way. She's never too concerned about what's behind her and typically focuses on the road ahead.

When we arrive at the park I let her off leash, so she can cut loose. Back on the leash, we head towards our main route. When we're outbound Cricket will run slightly behind me but when we turn for home she'll lead the way. Once home, she's treated to a snack. After her snack she'll drink water and head for bed, where she'll sleep for the next eight hours. A good life for sure!

A View from the Perch

What can Miss Cricket teach us about investing? Here are a few ideas we can learn from my favorite running partner.

Routines are important. An automated investment plan mixed in with an annual rebalance will treat you well over the long term. Cricket's morning routine rarely changes and she's a happy, healthy dog. For example, if you invested $10,000 into the Dimensional Core Equity I fund (DFEOX) 10 years ago, and routinely invested $100 per month, you'd now have over $42,000, an average annual return of 8.86%.[1]

Avoid distractions. Squirrels, birds, and other dogs try to derail Cricket from her objective, but she stays focused on her run. Investors today are bombarded with distractions from tweets, posts, chats, and snaps. The individual investor today is under a 24/7 media attack. Give your distraction a quick look and then move on to your goal. If you let your distractions get the better of you, you'll lose in the end. The Fidelity Magellan fund is a solid long-term performer. During the last 10 years, it averaged an annual return of 5.29%. However, some investors in this same fund averaged just .57%![2] Because they were distracted by outside noise they moved their money in and out of the fund. Had they stayed invested, they'd have improved their returns dramatically.

---

[1] Morningstar Office Hypothetical Tool, DFA Core Equity I, January 1, 2007 to January 31, 2017.
[2] Morningstar Office Fidelity Magellan Mutual Fund report, January 31, 2017.

Enjoy the treats. Cricket knows when she returns home she gets a dog treat. As an investor, it's advisable to take some money off the table and enjoy life. If you've accumulated an adequate nest egg, crack it open and spend some money. Is it time to take your dream vacation? Have you always wanted to own a second home? Do you feel called to donate to your favorite charity? After all, you can't take it with you when you die.

Sleep tight. Cricket sleeps like a rock without a care in the world. If your portfolio is keeping you up at night, sell some stocks to reduce your risk.

It's time to follow Cricket's lead. To be a better investor, focus on your investments, avoid distractions, and align your portfolio with your financial goals.

Happiness is a warm puppy. ~ Charles M. Schulz

February 27, 2017

Dow Jones = 20,837.43

91   And the Oscar Goes To...

The stars were aligning for *La La Land* until the unthinkable happened. Warren Beatty and Faye Dunaway announced The Best Picture Award Winner at the Oscars on Sunday Night – *La La Land*. The crowd, along with a few billion-people watching around the world, was stunned to find out the actual winner was *Moonlight*. Apparently, the accountant from Price Waterhouse Coopers was tweeting during the show and this may have caused the blunder.

Investors are constantly worried about making mistakes. Did I buy too late? Am I selling too early? What if the market goes down? What if interest rates go up? Investors can die a thousand deaths contemplating all the negative outcomes they might incur. Reacting to what might happen is often worse than what will happen to your portfolio's performance.

Here are four examples of investments that, at one or more points, looked like blunders. But because "buy and hold" investors held on, these investments became spectacular successes.

Blunder 1. An investor who purchased Apple in 1980 experienced a wild ride. During Apple's 37-year run it had 4 years when it lost more than 30% of its value, 2 years it lost 50% and 1 when it lost 70%! How did this "error" turn out? A

$10,000 investment in 1980 is now worth $2.8 million, giving the brave investor an average annual return of 16.91%![1]

Blunder 2. An investor who purchased the Vanguard 500 Index Fund (VFINX) on October 15, 1987, had to suffer through the worst one-day stock market correction in history. On October 19 the market fell 508 points, over 22%. How did this "gaffe" turn out? A $10,000 investment has grown to $147,000, providing an average annual return of 9.59%.[2]

Blunder 3. Amazon is crushing the competition and is on the brink of world dominance. It started trading in 1997. During this run, it had year-end losses of 15.83%, 22.18%, 30.47%, 44.65% and 79.56%, but Amazon has survived these major hits. How did an investor do if she bought Amazon in 1997? A $10,000 investment is now worth $4.2 million, providing an average annual return of 35.83%![3]

Blunder 4. An investor who purchased the iShares S&P 600 Small Cap Index fund (IJR) on August 1, 2007 lost 35% of her value in less than two years. But a $10,000 investment is now worth $23,000 for an average annual return of 9.12%.[4]

As these four examples reveal, it's possible to recover from a short-term investment error. We've all made mistakes in life.

---

[1] Morningstar Office Hypothetical Tool, February 28, 2017.
[2] Ibid.
[3] Ibid.
[4] Ibid.

A View from the Perch

If you fall, pick yourself up, dust yourself off, and move on. Time heals all wounds.

Here are a few suggestions to help you reduce your risk of making investment mistakes:

- Diversify your account with stocks, bonds and cash.
- Automate your monthly investments, which will help you purchase stocks in rising and falling markets.
- Have a cash position, which will soften the blow when stocks go down. When you experience a price drop, use your cash to buy more shares.
- Be patient and think long term.

The Hollywood elite will recover and I'm sure next year most everyone will have a good laugh over this year's most memorable Oscar moment.

Oscar and I have something in common. Oscar first came to the Hollywood scene in 1928. So did I. We're both a little weather-beaten, but we're still here and plan to be around for a whole lot longer. ~ - John Wayne, 1979 Academy Awards honoree

February 28, 2017

Dow Jones = 20,812.24

92   Balance

We are a people in pursuit of a work-life balance. We try to balance our diet, checkbooks, and car tires. It's impossible to ride a bike without balance, and scales must be balanced to get a true measure.

Investors should practice balance as well. Unfortunately, investors rarely pursue a balanced portfolio. They get too aggressive when markets rise and too conservative when they fall. Investors who practice the art of rebalancing will keep their risk level in check.

Let's look at a few brief moments in time to highlight this point.

1930. An investor who started 1930 with a portfolio of 50% stocks and 50% bonds saw her equity drop to 25% by 1932 and consisted of 25% stocks and 75% bonds, a mix too conservative for her long-term goals. In fact, it wasn't until 1949 that she regained her original allocation. She had to wait 19 years before her target allocation returned to normal.

2000. An investor who entered 2000 with a 50% stock and 50% bond portfolio saw his stock allocation drop to 29% by 2002. By the end of 2015, his portfolio was 35% stock and 65% in bonds, well below his original allocation of 50/50.

2009. An investor who started 2009 with a portfolio of 50% stock and 50% bonds now has a portfolio of 60% stock and 40% bonds by the end of 2010. By 2015 her stock allocation had risen to 65% and the bond portion dropped to 35%, too aggressive for her long-term goals.

As you can see, balance is seldom maintained. Investors must constantly battle the markets to keep their portfolio in line with their investment goals. If you do nothing, your portfolio will oscillate between too conservative and too aggressive.

Here are a few tips to help you stay focused on rebalancing your portfolio.

An annual rebalance is enough. Monthly or quarterly is too much.

Rebalance your accounts in January. This rebalance will allow you to take advantage of the prior year's movements. In addition, your dividends and capital gains will have been credited to your account.

Your 401(k) plan may have an automatic rebalancing tab or button allowing you to set it and forget it. The tab should have a few rebalancing options such as monthly, quarterly, or annually. An annual rebalance will work best.

It's easier to rebalance a portfolio of mutual funds or ETFs than it is one with individual stocks and bonds. It's not possible to sell a half share of stock or a third of a bond. If you plan to incorporate a rebalancing program in your portfolio, stick with funds.

It helps to automate the process so you can stick with your plan. It's emotionally hard to sell stocks when they're rising and buy bonds when they're falling. It's even harder to buy stocks when they're falling and sell bonds when they're rising. Leave your emotions at the door when you rebalance.

If you're a micro manager of your portfolio you can rebalance when your allocation moves 5% up or down. This strategy takes some work, but it can be done.

The key to long-term success is to match your financial goals to your investment portfolio. Once your hopes, dreams, and fears are identified, put your plan to work and rebalance yearly!

Life is like riding a bicycle. To keep your balance, you must keep moving. ~ Albert Einstein

March 8, 2017

Dow Jones = 20,855.73

93 How to Survive a Stock Market Correction

The Dow Jones Industrial Average continues to ascend to new heights. The higher it climbs, the more noise you'll hear about a correction. At some point those calling for a correction will be right. Corrections are typical and occur about every three to five years. A bear (down) market will last about 18 months while a bull (up) market will run for about 8 years.[1]

How can you protect yourself against a bear market attack?

Don't panic! A market drop is normal. Painful, but normal.

Don't make any changes initially. Let the market correction find its footing before you make any major adjustments to your portfolio.

Cash is king. If you have a cash cushion you're less likely to make rash decisions regarding your stock holdings. How much cash? My recommendation is for you to hold two to three years' worth of expenses in cash. If your annual expenses are $50,000, then your cash amount should be in the range of $100,000 to $150,000.

Diversify your assets. A balanced portfolio of stocks, bonds, cash, and alternative investments will help cushion the blow

---

[1] https://www.forbes.com/sites/robertlenzner/2015/01/02/bull-markets-last-five-times-longer-than-bear-markets/#4b26d84a2dd5, Robert Lenzer, January 2, 2015, accessed March 10, 2017.

from a market drop. During a drop it's likely bonds will perform well. During the 2008 market mauling long-term U.S. government bonds rose 25.9%.[2]

Rebalance your portfolio. Rebalancing will allow you to take advantage of lower stock prices and keep both your risk level and asset allocation in check.

Eliminate your margin balance. A sure way to lose more than you can afford is to use leverage. If you've tapped the margin in your account to buy securities, I'd encourage you to eliminate it entirely. The best way to make a bad situation worse is to use margin in a down market.

Stay invested. During the two days following the crash of October 19, 1987 the Dow Jones Industrial Average rose 16%. Despite the dramatic drop of Black Monday, the Dow ended 1987 with a gain and has since risen 1,100%.

Look for bargains. Is it possible your favorite stock is now 25% or 50% cheaper? If you're not sure what to purchase, focus on a broad-based index fund. An index fund will allow you to gain market exposure with the click of your mouse.

Think long term. A bear market lasts about 18 months. It's likely you'll own your investments for years, maybe decades, before you'll need the money. Thinking generationally will help get you through the dark days of a market downturn.

---

[2] Dimensional Fund Advisors 2016 Matrix Book.

Markets recover. The stock market has always recovered – always!

Have fun. The market will go up, down, and sideways long after we're gone. Instead of marinating in a stew of worry get outside and enjoy your friends, family, and hobbies.

Stock market corrections come and go. The market is a long-term wealth-creation machine that is occasionally interrupted with a pullback. If you stick to these tips, you'll have an opportunity to benefit from the market's long-term performance.

I never attempt to make money on the stock market. I buy on the assumption that they could close the market the next day and not reopen it for five years. ~ Warren Buffett

March 10, 2017

Dow Jones = 20,902.98

94   Worse than a Stock Market Correction?

Investors constantly scan the horizon looking for a stock market correction. While they sit on their front porches anticipating a correction they leave their back doors wide open to potential estate problems. Stock market crashes can be temporarily painful, but a poor estate plan can cause permanent damage to your wealth.

Individuals spend most of their free financial time focusing on stocks, bonds, and funds and pay little attention to their estate. It's not easy to ponder your mortality but it's necessary if you want to protect your hard-earned dollars for your family.

Here are a few areas that can bring heartache to your heirs.

No will or trust. If you die without a will or trust, it's possible to lose 40% of your estate to the federal government in the form of an estate tax. In addition to your tax loss, your remaining estate may end up in the wrong hands. A client of mine inherited $4 million from his rich uncle who died without proper estate documents and he had to write a $2 million check to the IRS for estate taxes.

No life insurance. Individuals who own little or no life insurance run the risk of losing their assets to creditors in the event of death. I've talked to several people who don't insure the stay-at-home spouse. The breadwinner assumes, incorrectly, he'll be able to take care of his home financially if the non-breadwinner spouse passes away. How much life insurance is enough? At a minimum, you should own enough to pay off all your debts, provide for your spouse's lifetime income, and fund your children's college education.

No long-term care (LTC) insurance. This insurance coverage is becoming a must-have item. The average monthly cost for staying in a long-term care facility is about $5,000 and the average stay is about four years. If you and your spouse enter a LTC facility at the same time, it's possible you could spend $480,000 or more. If you have a high level of investments, you might not need LTC insurance. However, if you use your assets to pay for LTC your family will be left to live without them.

No beneficiary. It takes about two minutes to update the beneficiary information on your retirement accounts and insurance policies. A beneficiary designation overrides all your estate documents, including your family will and trust. This might not be an issue if you're happily married and don't have any children. However, if you're divorced and you forget to update your beneficiary information, then your assets may end up in the hands of your ex-spouse!

No umbrella liability policy. This is a cost-effective way to protect your property. The cost of adding more insurance coverage to your property and casualty policy is minimal. A house with a pool or horses or some other attraction should have an umbrella liability policy.

A solid financial and estate foundation will help protect your assets while you're living and long after you're gone. I recommend spending some time updating your insurance and estate planning documents. After all, an ounce of provision is worth a pound of cure.

I have seen something else under the sun: The race is not to the swift or the battle to the strong, nor does food come to the wise or wealth to the brilliant or favor to the learned; but time and chance happen to them all. ~ Ecclesiastes 9:11

March 21, 2017

Dow Jones = 20,668

95   Shaw's Cove

Shaw's Cove is a beautiful slice of paradise located in Laguna Beach, and my friends and I spent a fair amount of time there during our summer vacations.

We'd walk to Shaw's equipped with three items: boogie board, snorkeling gear, and smashball. Throughout the day we'd use all three. When the waves were up we'd ride our boogie boards. If they weren't, we'd go snorkeling. When we got tired of being in the water (a rare event) we'd play smashball. We'd repeat this process until we got hungry. Our strategy prepared us well for all beach conditions. It was our version of being diversified.

An investor should be prepared for all types of market conditions as well by owning investments for growth, income, and safety.

Stocks are owned for growth. They'll be your long-term wealth generating machine. The S&P 500 Index has generated an average annual return of 10% from 1926 to 2015.[1]

Bonds are owned for income and safety. They're boring but stable. And they can also play a significant part in increasing your family's wealth. They pay predictable monthly, quarterly, or annual income. When stocks fall, bonds usually rally. U.S. Government Bonds have averaged 5.6% from 1926 to 2015.[2]

---

[1] Dimensional Fund Advisors Matrix Book 2016.
[2] Ibid.

Cash is owned for safety. It's always nice to have some dry powder. Cash is safe and liquid. If you need access to capital, look no further than cash. When stocks or bonds fall, it's nice to have cash on hand so you can buy the dip. It can also help you ride out a stock market correction. With a strong cash position, you can afford to hold onto your stocks while they recover. From 1926 to 2015, cash, as measured by the U.S. T-Bill, has averaged a return of 3.4% per year.[3]

Stocks, bonds, and cash are the cornerstone of a solid portfolio. These three instruments work in concert to balance your portfolio. If you own more stocks than bonds, you're a growth-oriented investor. If you own more bonds than stocks, you're a conservative investor.

A portfolio with 70% stocks, 25% bonds, and 5% cash generated an average annual return of 8.57% from 1926 to 2015. A $10,000 investment thus allocated in 1926 is now worth $15 million.

A portfolio with 50% stocks, 35% bonds, and 15% cash generated an average annual return of 7.47% from 1926 to 2015. A $10,000 investment in 1926 is now worth $6 million.

A portfolio with 30% stocks, 50% bonds, and 20% cash generated an average annual return of 6.48% from 1926 to 2015. A $10,000 investment in 1926 is now worth $2.6 million.

---

[3] Ibid.

As you can see, the more stock you own, the greater your long-term wealth. But remember, it's important to match your asset allocation to your financial plan and goals. When your investments are in line with your goals, you're more likely to stick with your plan over the long haul.

I could not help concluding this man had the most supreme pleasure while he was driven so fast and so smoothly by the sea. ~ Captain James Cook

March 23, 2017

Dow Jones = 20,656.58

96 By the People, For the People?

President Trump and House Speaker Paul Ryan pulled the plug on their Republican health care bill. The same week, Chuck Schumer encouraged his fellow Democrats to filibuster Neil Gorsuch, the nominee for the U.S. Supreme Court. Politics as usual.

Democrats and Republicans have been adversaries since March 4, 1797 when John Adams was elected as the second president of the United States. The parties have been butting heads for 220 years and despite their best (worst) efforts, our economy and stock market continue to march on. I'm afraid their bickering and whining may carry on for another 220 years.

On CNBC, commentators, money managers, traders, and other experts were predicting that the stock market would fall on the news the health care bill had flatlined. The experts painted a bleak future for Trump's presidency because it was dead on arrival. They opined that this news didn't bode well for the other items on his agenda.

As far as your investments are concerned, does it matter what our elected officials pass or don't pass? Does it matter if they fail to reach a compromise on important issues? Does it matter who is in the White House? Congress? The Senate? No. In the long run, what happens in Washington D.C., matters little to your portfolio.

A View from the Perch

It took our elected officials 76 years to abolish slavery, 131 years to allow women to vote, 175 years to pass the Civil Rights Bill, and 201 years to pass the American's with Disabilities Act. Can you imagine how much stronger our country (world) would be today if our politicians had been working for the people since 1789?

Robert Shiller has been tracking stock prices from 1871. In 1871 the index was at 4.44 and Friday the S&P 500 closed at 2,438.98 a gain of 54,831%![1] The invisible hand of the market continues to rule the day.

Try to ignore goings on inside The Beltway. Instead, spend time on what does matter to your financial future by listening to the gurus such as Tim Cook, Warren Buffett, John Bogle, Fred Smith, Sheryl Sandberg, and Robert Johnson who will tell you all you need to know about our economy and the state of America. Politicians forever take money out of your pocket. Why not let these business leaders put some back in? Elected officials come and go. When the market does fall because of what happens in D.C., use it as an opportunity to buy the dip.

Here are a few tips you can use when constructing your investment portfolio to put yourself in a position to win.

---

[1] http://www.econ.yale.edu/~shiller/data.htm, Robert Shiller, Long term stock, bond, interest rate, and consumption data accessed March 26, 2017.

Create your financial plan. It will be your guide. Your plan will reflect your hopes, dreams, and fears and will help you direct your investments.

Invest in stocks. The stock market will be your best friend over time. Investing in low-cost index funds or high-quality stocks should be the cornerstone of your portfolio.

Automate your investing. When your investments are automated you're less likely to stop investing due to political noise.

Rebalance your investment portfolio on an annual basis. This will help reduce your risk and keep your portfolio in balance with your goals.

Invest early and often. The earlier you start investing the more money you'll have in your account later in life.

Spend less than you earn. The more you can save, the better your financial position.

Avoid excess debt. Your total monthly debt payments should be less than 38% of your gross income. If your gross income is $10,000 per month, your debt payments should not exceed $3,800.

Give money away. Do some good with the money you've accumulated because of your well-planned and sensible investing.

A View from the Perch

You can find good reasons to scuttle your equities in every morning paper and on every broadcast of the nightly news. ~ Peter Lynch

March 26, 2017

Dow Jones = 20,550.98

97   What's the YTB?

"What's the YTB?" an elder broker bellowed from the back of the conference room.

"5%!" responded the wholesaler.

"Sweet!" answered the broker, "I'll sell your fund!"

I was attending one of my first branch meetings as a newly minted broker and had never heard the term YTB. I had heard of other yield acronyms like YTM, yield-to-maturity, and YTC, yield-to-call, but not YTB.

The YTB is referred to as the yield-to-broker. It's the fee the broker was going to get paid for selling the mutual fund. He didn't care about the features or benefits; his only concern was what he was going to get paid for selling the product to his clients.

Brokerage and insurance products are sold, not bought. Brokerage firms and insurance companies are product manufacturing machines. Their product creativity and distribution system is without peer. They have a vested interest in selling you their products. These firms may earn a commission when you buy their fund and they'll receive an ongoing fee as long as you own it.

When you purchase a product from a brokerage firm or insurance company, it's buyer beware. It may have a front-end commission where the fee is deducted from your investment or it may have a back-end sales charge that is triggered when you sell your fund. It's important to read the small print before you commit your capital to a new investment.

When I started my own advisory firm, I had a visit from a life insurance agent who wanted to show me a permanent life insurance product. It was a $1 million policy with an annual premium of $100,000 for 10 years. I asked him what his commission was going to be if a client bought it. He replied that the first-year commission would be $55,000. I stopped listening to his sales pitch after he told me what his fee was going to be, and we haven't done any business together.

As you invest your hard-earned dollars take time to ask questions about the fees you'll be paying. Here are a few questions to get you started.

- How do you get paid?
- What is the fee or commission on this product?
- Is there a penalty for selling early? How early?
- Are there any other fees?
- How does this fee compare to other fees?
- Do you own this same investment?
- Does your mother own this same investment?
- Are there investments with lower fees?
- Does the fee go down if I invest more money?
- Keep an eye on your costs. The lower your fees, the higher your returns.

Honest scales and balances belong to the Lord; all the weights in the bag are of his making. ~ Proverbs 16:11

A View from the Perch

March 27, 2017

Dow Jones = 20,550.98

98 Should You Follow Your Dreams?

At the age of 50, I started my own company. It's been an exciting, nerve-racking adventure. My daughter was leaving for college and my wife was working part time at our church. I had doubts, anxiety, and fear and wondered if I'd made the correct choice. I had considered other options, like staying with my large corporate employer forever or retiring early to join the mission field. In the end, because it had been a lifelong dream, I launched my own company.

For the Spirit God gave us does not make us timid, but gives us power, love and self-discipline. ~ 2 Timothy 1:7

I had some case history and a path to follow. My maternal grandfather started his own company when he was 50. Instead of having one daughter in college he had three, and his wife didn't work. He had a successful business career and a better one as a philanthropist.

Be strong and courageous. Do not be afraid or terrified because of them, for the Lord your God goes with you; he will never leave you nor forsake you. ~ Deuteronomy 31:6

While in college, two of my friends and I bought the rights to a company that produced calendars and we became business owners! I learned more about business by owning our little company than all the business courses I took. We had to deal with printers, photographers, models, retail outlets, customers, suppliers, etc. I loved it! I knew I wanted my own business but didn't realize it would be another 30 years before my dream would come true. Oh well, better late than never!

Yet we urge you, brothers and sisters, to do so more and more, and to make it your ambition to lead a quiet life: You should mind your own business and work with your hands, just as we told you, so that your daily life may win the respect of outsiders and so that you will not be dependent on anybody. ~ 1 Thessalonians 4:10–13

If you're ready to burn your boat and start your own company, be prepared for a mountain of negativity and threats. Most people won't have the courage, wisdom, or vision to start a company. Don't listen to the naysayers. You may receive threats from your current employer but trudge on and concentrate on your goal. Others will think you're crazy. They'll say you're too young or too old. They'll wonder how you'll support yourself or attract clients. The list of negatives will grow proportionally to the number of people you talk to. Regardless, do it any way!

They will have no fear of bad news; their hearts are steadfast, trusting in the Lord. Their hearts are secure, they will have no fear; in the end, they will look in triumph on their foes. They have freely scattered their gifts to the poor, their righteousness endures forever; their horn will be lifted high in honor. ~ Psalm 112:7–9

If you have visions of starting your own company, here are a few tips to get you started.

There is no perfect plan or time to start your business. A good plan today is better than a perfect plan tomorrow. If you wait for all the stars to align, you'll never start your own business.

There has never been a better time in the history of the world to start your own business. The technology today gives you the power to reach billions of people with the click of a mouse. The barriers to entry for most businesses are extremely low and access to capital is tremendously high.

If you're young, take advantage of your youth and enthusiasm. An ideal time to start a business is when you don't have other commitments like a spouse, children, or a mortgage. You're free and nimble to pursue your dream.

If you work for a large corporation, honor your employment contract and agreement. If you're not sure about the big legal words in your contract, hire an attorney who specializes in contract law to help guide you in your decision. Despite your best efforts it's possible your former employer will sue you. So be prepared to spend the dollars necessary to defend your good name.

Focus on what you do best and hire others to fill in the gaps.

Enjoy your journey. Listen to the words of A.A. Milne, "Rivers know this: there is no hurry. We shall get there some day."

Have fun. You'll experience trials and tribulations but at the end of the day it's your business with your name on the door. And what could be better than that?

Therefore, I tell you, do not worry about your life... ~ Matthew 6:25

April 1, 2017

Dow Jones = 20,663.22

99   Spring Cleaning

Snow is melting. Flowers are blooming. Grass is growing. Robins are singing. Spring has arrived! So, it's now time for a little spring cleaning. After months of dark days and cold nights, open some windows and let the fresh air and sunshine into your home.

When my family and I lived in Connecticut, we loved the arrival of spring. Once the snow melted we'd put our yard back together. We'd pick up branches and tree limbs. We'd clear flower beds and add layers of mulch. On the inside, we'd open several windows and let the fresh spring air whip through our house to force stale winter air out.

Your investment portfolio may need some spring cleaning as well. The arrival of spring also marks the end of the first quarter. Hopefully you're closer to achieving your financial goals.

Here a few spring cleaning tips for your investment portfolio review:

- If you're holding a losing investment, it may be time to sell it and move the money into a new idea. Prune your portfolio as you prune your garden.
- Do you need to trim some gains? If you have an investment worth more than 10%, 20%, or 30%

or more of your account, it's time to take some profits.
- Is it time to rebalance your portfolio? Doing so will help reduce your risk and keep your original asset allocation intact. For example, if in 2009 you had started with a portfolio of 50% stocks and 50% bonds, today your mix may be 70% stocks and 30% bonds. The market has soared since 2009 and, as a result, your allocation is not aligned with your original goal. Rebalancing will fix this problem.
- Spring is a glorious time to finish an outdoor project. Adding a deck, pool, or barbeque to your home may enhance the value. Adding small, international, or real estate companies to your portfolio may give it a boost.
- Do you need to update your will? Has your family grown? Have you added a new asset? With the arrival of spring and the departure of tax season, spend some time updating your estate documents.
- Create a financial plan. A well-constructed plan will help you with your annual spring cleaning. It will allow you to focus on your long-term goals with an occasional trim here and there.

A View from the Perch

Sitting on a deck under sunny skies is an excellent backdrop for the review of your portfolio. A small change today can bear much fruit tomorrow.

For behold, the winter is past; the rain is over and gone. The flowers appear on the earth, the time of singing has come, and the voice of the turtledove is heard in our land. ~ Song of Solomon 2:11–12

April 10, 2017

Dow Jones = 20,658.01

100 Say What?

I spent most of my youth playing football. I played it in junior high, high school, and college. Our playbooks included diagrams and words not legible to the non-footballer. Some of the plays were "I right 30-trap," "trips right 382," or "Alabama 99." Each one had a different meaning and purpose. After it was called, each player knew their specific assignments. The language became second nature to everyone on the team because we practiced constantly.

My friends and I would play pickup games at the park when we weren't playing organized football. The play calling for these games was simple and clear. I might tell Steve to run towards the hippo water fountain and Randy to run at the rocket. Dave might run to the dead grass spot and then towards the swing set.

Watching CNBC this past week I was alternatively amused and horrified with the language used to describe various investments and investment strategies. Here's a sample.

"We're tactically allocating our risk assets to deliver alpha to our high net worth clients by purchasing high beta cyclical names." What? Here's my interpretation of what was said, "We are buying profitable stocks, so we can make money for our clients."

"We're removing risk assets from our satellite portfolio by purchasing low volatility, negatively correlated assets." Huh? I would have said we're buying bonds.

"We're going to deleverage our non-liquid, alternative assets and transition the proceeds to our short-term liquid account." Come again? I think they meant to say they're selling assets and then depositing the money into their cash account.

Wall Street lingo is designed to confuse the masses. The wolves use big words and fancy wrappers to sell high commission products to the sheep. At the end of the day, there are only three things you can do with your money. You can invest for growth, income, or safety. If you're investing for growth, buy stocks. If you need income, buy bonds. If you crave safety, keep your money in cash.

As you construct your portfolio ask yourself which investments you need to own so you can achieve your goals. Focus on simple investment strategies with clear language and hold them for the long haul. Capisce?

Come, let us go down and confuse their language so they will not understand each other. ~ Genesis 11:7

April 13, 2017

Dow Jones = 20,453.25

101   Time to Play It Safe?

In 1926, Mrs. Moats invested three dollars in separate investments. She placed a dollar coin in each of three boxes with strict instructions not to open them until December 31, 2015. She invested one dollar in large company stocks for her "risky" box. Her next dollar was invested in a "safe" portfolio of U.S. Treasury Bonds. In the third box, she kept her dollar in cash just in case boxes 1 and 2 became worthless.

After the coins were placed in their respective boxes she buried them in her backyard.

On December 31, 2015, her grandchildren dug up the boxes to see how well her investments had performed. With all the trouble and turmoil during the past 89 years, her grandchildren were convinced the safe investments had performed best. Here's how each dollar fared.

Box 1 – Large Company Stocks. Her $1 investment is now worth $5,386. This portfolio returned 10% per year. Her "risky" portfolio endured several years with negative returns and extreme volatility, but it dramatically outperformed her "safe" investments.[1]

Box 2 – U.S. Treasury Bonds. Her $1 investment is now worth $21.[2] Her "safe" portfolio averaged an annual return of 3.4%.

---

[1] Dimensional Fund Advisors 2016 Matrix Book.
[2] Ibid.

It made money every year and never produced a negative return.

Box 3 – Cash. Her 1926 dollar is now worth about 8 cents. It's purchasing power has been eroded by inflation which averaged 2.9% per year during this 89-year stretch.[3]

The U.S. stock market is near an all-time high. By some measures it's fairly valued, if not overvalued. The public outcry for a stock market correction is increasing as the market climbs higher. Is it time to play it safe? Should you sell your stocks and move your money to cash? In the short term, this strategy may appear prudent as it would be nice to avoid another stock market correction.

Here are a few things to consider before you sell your growth-oriented investments.

When should you sell your stocks? Today? Tomorrow? Next week? How will you know when it's the best time to sell? If you sold them before last year's presidential election you missed a 16% return.

If you sell your stocks, when do you buy them back? How will you know when it's safe to get back into the market? If you were fortunate enough to sell your stocks prior to the 2008 Great Recession, but failed to get back into the market, you missed out on a 192% gain.

---

[3] Ibid.

If you decide to keep your money in cash, you'll lose money to taxes and inflation. At the end of five years the purchasing power of your dollar will lose about 15%. In 1988 I could purchase four U.S. postage stamps for a dollar. Today I can only buy two. [4]

A buy and hold strategy based on your financial plan is smart. Owning stocks for the long haul will give you the best opportunity to achieve generational wealth.

For whoever has will be given more, and they will have an abundance... ~ Matthew 25:29

April 17, 2017

Dow Jones = 20,636.91

---

[4] https://about.usps.com/who-we-are/postal-history/domestic-letter-rates-since-1863.pdf, Historian U.S. Postal Service, accessed April 21, 2017.

102 Storage Wars

Driving around my extended neighborhood I noticed several large storage units. A quick Google search for storage units near my house netted 20 facilities, with more being built. Storage units cater to people who suffer from affluenza or hoarding. If you depend on a storage facility, you may have too much junk and it's time for you to part company with your once-precious items. If you've watched an episode or two of "Storage Wars," you know people covet some crazy items. However, most of the items are common things like bed frames, mattresses, dresser-drawers, mirrors, and other household goods. Do you still need to keep your TV trays, eight-track tape player, or rotary phone?

In financial terms, more stuff means higher expenses. The higher your household expenses are, the more assets you'll need to retire. The math is simple. If your annual expenses are $50,000, you'll need about $2 million in assets to retire. Reducing your expenses will give you the opportunity to retire sooner with fewer assets. For every $10,000 in expenses you can eliminate equates to $250,000 less in assets.

Here are a few tips to help you dig out from your pile of stuff.

Take an inventory of the items you want to keep and the items you need to keep.

Donate those items you no longer need to your favorite charity. This will help others in need and give you a tax deduction.

Sell your items at a garage sale. One man's trash is another man's treasure. Can you generate a few extra dollars from your swag?

Eliminate the storage unit. A 10 x 10 climate-controlled storage unit will cost about $175 per month or $2,100 per year.

Are you an empty nester? Can you reduce your household footprint? Downsizing to a smaller home will take a huge chunk out of your expenses. A smaller home yields less stuff.

Save your money. After you've eliminated some expenses invest your savings. Let's say you can save $500 per month because of your cost cutting. Investing $500 per month at 7% will be worth about $86,500 in 10 years.

Start today and don't procrastinate. The sooner you start digging through your pile of things, the better your financial future will be! My wife and I attacked our excess a few years ago and it was liberating. The freedom we received from having less junk and lower expenses has allowed us to do more with less.

Do not store up for yourselves treasures on earth… ~ Matthew 6:19

April 19, 2017

Dow Jones = 20,404.49

103   No Fear

Fear and worry are paralyzing. When I jump in to the ocean, I fully expect to get eaten by a shark, especially if I go swimming during the Discovery Channel's Shark Week. When I hike in the mountains I know I'll have to fight off a slew of bears. In Texas, every stick is a rattle snake. Of course, my fears are unfounded. I've never been bitten by a shark, fought with a bear, or stepped on a rattle snake. But fear of the unknown can keep us from enjoying life.

A person has a 1 in 3.7 million chance of being killed by a shark. The odds of dying from the flu are 1 in 63.[1] Sharks, alligators, and bears each kill about one person per year, according to a 2015 Washington Post article. Venomous snakes and lizards kill around six people annually. Approximately 48 people are killed by a cow or dog each year.[2]

A Bible search for the words "fear" and "worry" produced 351 results.[3] Most verses with fear and worry are preceded by "do not" as in do not fear or do not worry.

---

[1] http://natgeotv.com/ca/human-shark-bait/facts, accessed April 27, 2017.

[2] https://www.washingtonpost.com/news/wonk/wp/2015/06/16/chart-the-animals-that-are-most-likely-to-kill-you-this-summer/?utm_term=.e46cacf09197, Christopher Ingraham, June 16, 2015, accessed April 27, 2017.

[3] https://www.biblegateway.com/, accessed April 27, 2017.

So do not fear, for I am with you; do not be dismayed, for I am your God. I will strengthen you and help you; I will uphold you with my righteous right hand. ~ Isaiah 41:10

Therefore do not worry about tomorrow, for tomorrow will worry about itself. Each day has enough trouble of its own. ~ Matthew 6:34

Investors appear to live in a constant state of worry and fear. Here are a few suggestions for overcoming some common investment concerns.

Fear of a stock market correction. Diversify your assets to limit your exposure to a correction. Investing in bonds, small companies, real estate, gold, and international investments will cushion the blow from a correction. These additional asset classes would have reduced your losses by 44% during the 2008 stock market correction when compared to an all-stock investment portfolio.[4]

Fear of running out of money. Longevity risk is a concern. To help avoid it, invest in stocks. The stock market has produced a 10% average annual return since 1926 while the bond market generated a return of 5.6%. $1 invested in stocks is now worth $5,386. $1 in bonds is worth $132. The performance of stocks has outperformed bonds by a ratio of 40 to 1![5]

---

[4] Morningstar Office Hypothetical Tool.
[5] 2016 Dimensional Funds Matrix Book.

Fear of rising interest rates. Rising rates will lower bond prices. Create a bond ladder to protect yourself from falling prices. A portfolio of bonds maturing every year will allow you to invest in both short and long-term bonds. When a short-term bond matures, invest the proceeds in a new bond with a higher interest rate.

Fear of missing out. FOMO is real! Don't chase returns on a high-flying stock. If you want to buy a stock after it has appreciated significantly, wait for it to pull back before committing capital.

Do not let fear keep you from achieving your financial dreams. Plan for your future and good things can happen.

The only thing we have to fear is fear itself. ~ FDR

April 28, 2017

Dow Jones = 20,940.51

104 Nothing but Net!

One of the best sounds in basketball is "swish" as the ball passes through the net. I love watching long-range shooters drain effortless, smooth three-pointers. Some of the best shooters in the game have been Larry Bird, Kobe Bryant, and Steph Curry. My favorite long-range shooter was Meadowlark Lemon of the Harlem Globetrotters.

My friends and I used to play H-O-R-S-E at the local park. Our shots were creative and crazy. The stakes went up when one of us would call a swish shot. The basket wouldn't count if the ball hit the backboard or the rim.

Investing has its own version of "nothing but net." Gross returns are impressive, but you can only spend net returns. To calculate your net return, you must subtract inflation, taxes and fees. The net return is what you can spend to buy food, gas, and other household items.

Let's review some net returns.

Stocks. The gross return on stocks from 1926 has been 10%. This is impressive, especially when compounded over 90 years. Inflation during this time averaged 2.9%. Subtracting inflation, the return falls to 7.1%. Minus a 28% tax rate lowers your return to 5.1%. If you work with an advisor who charges 1%, your net return is now 4.1%. Netting out inflation, taxes, and fees, your 10% gross return cascades 59% to 4.1%. A $10,000 investment in stocks will grow to $372,000 over 90 years with a net return of 4.1%.

Bonds. Long-term government bonds averaged 5.6% for 90 years. Inflation reduced this by 2.9%. Subtracting inflation, taxes, and fees, your net return is now .94%. A $10,000 investment in bonds is now worth $23,200.

Cash. Cash's return will leave a hole in your wallet. The one-month U.S. Treasury Bill has averaged 3.4% since 1926. Subtracting inflation, taxes, and fees ,your net return drops to a negative .64%. A $10,000 "investment" in cash is now worth $5,611.

You need to own stocks to create generational wealth. An overabundance of bonds and cash is an air ball. I recommend keeping a large portion of your portfolio in stocks, so you can stay ahead of inflation, taxes, and fees.

I hate to lose more than I like to win. ~ Larry Bird

May 7, 2017

Dow Jones = 21,102.27

105 What's an Emerging Market Anyway?

The talk around the water cooler lately has been about investing internationally – specifically in emerging markets. What does "emerging" mean anyway? Webster's Dictionary describes emerging as "newly created or noticed and growing in strength or popularity, becoming widely known or established." Sounds good to me, but what does it have to do with investing? Plenty.

Most investors invest in established, developed markets like the United States, United Kingdom, Germany, Japan, Australia, or Canada. These markets have several things in common, such as contract law, stable governments, and a modern infrastructure. Citizens of these countries reap the benefits of a modern society by spending their wealth on fine dining, big screen TVs, huge homes, and expensive cars. Clean water and (mostly) affordable health care is available to all.

Emerging markets include the BRICs: Brazil, Russia, India, and China. Other underdeveloped markets include Peru, Thailand, South Africa, Chile, and Turkey. These countries typically have unstable governments, poor infrastructure, and impoverished citizens.

I've had the good fortune to travel to a few emerging markets like Hungary, Haiti, Nicaragua, and Mexico. In Haiti, the poverty is inconceivable. Corruption in the government has left its citizens in misery. Homes, roads, and cars are in disrepair. Unfortunately, it will be centuries before Haiti is an emerging market.

Why should you invest in an emerging market? A good reason is because they're emerging. They're growing. A growing middle class is giving these people access to things we take for granted like jobs, microwaves, washers, dryers, and iPhones. It's also giving them hope. As these markets begin to prosper, so will their citizens.

How much of your portfolio should you allocate to emerging markets? I recommend 5% to 10%. Here are three popular funds you should consider.

- Dimensional Funds Emerging Markets Portfolio (DFEMX). Year to date it's up 17.91%.
- Vanguard FTSE Emerging Markets Index Fund (VWO). Year to date it's up 12.94%.
- IShares MSCI Emerging Markets ETF (EEM). Year to date it's up 14.42%.

The 2017 returns for these funds are outperforming the Standard & Poor's 500 index. However, emerging markets are risky, and the volatility is high. The standard deviation for emerging markets is 28.7. By comparison, developed markets have a standard deviation of 17.4, a 65% difference![1] In 1998, Turkey's market returned 252% while Russia lost 83%. Last year Brazil was up 67% and Egypt was down 11.4%.[2] The

---

[1] Morningstar Office 2017 Market Assumptions.
[2] Dimensional Funds 2017 Matrix Book.

divergence in returns from year to year is vast. Therefore, an allocation of just 5% to 10% makes sense for most investors.

As you construct your portfolio add a pinch of emerging markets. It could give your portfolio a boost.

It's a small world, but I wouldn't want to paint it. ~ Steven Wright

May 13, 2017

Dow Jones = 20,981.93

106   Who Wants to Be a Millionaire?

"Who Wants to Be a Millionaire" is an entertaining game show once hosted by Regis Philbin (cue theme song). It gave contestants a chance to win a million dollars if they correctly answered a series of multiple choice questions. If they needed help, they could tap a lifeline or call on the audience.

You can play your own version of "Who Wants to Be a Millionaire" in the stock market. Its long-term trend will give you the opportunity to accumulate wealth – if you play correctly.

Time is your friend if you want to accumulate wealth. The earlier you start investing, the sooner you'll achieve your goal. If a 25-year-old wants to retire at age 55 with a million dollars, she must save $442 per month. If she waits until age 35, she must save $1,316 per month. If she waits until age 45, she must save $4,881 per month.

Dollar cost averaging is a proven strategy to accumulate wealth. Using this method, save the same dollar amount each month and invest it in a fund of your choice. To increase your odds of success, automate your savings. An automatic dollar cost averaging program will keep you invested in good times and bad.

Let's look at investing $500 a month in the Vanguard S&P 500 Index Fund (VFINX) for 10, 20, 30, and 40 years.

A $500 monthly investment for 10 years yielded a total value of $131,596. The average annual return was 10.73%. (April 2007–April 2017)

A $500 monthly investment for 20 years accumulated $320,243 for an average annual return of 7.73%. (April 1997–April 2017)

A $500 monthly investment for 30 years grew to $1.04 million for an average annual return of 9.26%. (April 1987–April 2017)

A $500 monthly investment for 40 years resulted in $4.16 million for an average annual return of 10.87%. (April 1977–April 2017)

As you can see, time in the market wins! As Nick Murray once said, "The best time to invest money is when you have it and the best time to sell is when you need the money." You can control your savings and expenses. The more you save and the less you pay means more wealth for you and your family.

Someone is sitting in the shade today because someone planted a tree a long time ago. ~ Warren Buffett

May 15, 2017

Dow Jones = 20,981.93

107 Don't Read This If You're Under 50!

Turning 50 is a huge milestone and an exciting time. Age 50 is considered the gateway to the golden years with much to look forward to because you still have another 31 years to live, according to your projected life expectancy. The pressure to look and act cool also wanes as you grow older. If you want to wear sweaters with shorts or sandals with socks, go for it. If you want to eat dinner at 4:00 and be in bed by 8:00, knock yourself out. If you want to wear a big floppy hat, wraparound sunglasses, long sleeve shirts, and cover yourself in zinc oxide before heading off to the beach, who's going to stop you?

Age 50 is also the time when most individuals get serious about retirement planning. A person 49 years, 11 months, and 29 days old has little interest in retirement planning. When he turns 50 he freaks out because retirement is now on the horizon. 65 is still the preferred retirement age for many workers, so turning 50 means there are only 15 more years until he rides off into the sunset. Fifteen years isn't a long time, and this is what makes him nervous.

By age 50 you should have 5 times your annual salary saved, according to a report by CNBC.[1] If your annual income is $100,000 you should have $500,000 in savings. Congratulations to you if you've achieved this milestone. If

---

[1] http://www.cnbc.com/2017/02/22/heres-how-much-money-you-should-have-saved-at-every-age.html, Kathleen Elkins, February 22, 2017.

your current asset level falls short, have no fear because you still have time to salvage a comfortable retirement.

Once you turn 50 you can contribute more money to your retirement accounts. The government allows you to invest an extra $1,000 to your IRA and an additional $6,000 to your 401(k). These additional savings will help you make up for lost time.

As you march through the golden years, here are a few things to consider:

- Health is wealth. It pays to take care of yourself. As you age, time and gravity are working against you, so focus on eating well and working out. Eating fruits, vegetables, and anything that swims or flies will be good for the ticker. Hit the gym and put in a few miles on the road to get some quality exercise. According to the American Academy of Family Physicians, exercise helps prevent chronic disease and improves your mood.[2]
- Help others. A benefit of aging is that you're able to help others spiritually, emotionally, and financially. It's time to put your wisdom and resources to work.

---

[2] https://www.agingcare.com/articles/exercise-benefits-for-the-elderly-95383.htm, Marlo Sollitto, accessed May 20, 2017.

- Give. A philanthropic plan will pay dividends for you and others. A thoughtful giving plan will help others for many years while giving you income and estate tax benefits.
- Pursue your dreams. Do you want to start a business? Explore distant lands? Try a new hobby? The golden years are a perfect time for you to start checking off items on your bucket list.
- Own stocks. They'll help you grow your wealth and generate more income. Stocks will also help you offset the effects of inflation. You need to own assets that will grow over time so your purchasing power grows or stays constant. A 3% inflation rate will lower your purchasing power by 59% over a 30-year period. A dollar today will be worth 41 cents in 30 years.

Aging is a benefit not afforded to many, so enjoy the ride. Live your golden years with spunk and gusto. Live your life to the fullest so you have no regrets when Gabriel blows his horn.

How old would you be if you didn't know how old you were? ~ Satchel Paige

May 21, 2017

Dow Jones = 20,894.83

108 A Better Alternative?

Alternative investments, in theory, are designed to rise if your traditional stock and bond portfolio falls. They're supposed to zig when your stocks zag. An alternative investment is considered anything other than a traditional investment like a stock or bond and comes in many forms, such as real estate investment trusts, gold ETFs, or managed futures. Publicly traded alternative investments are an affordable way to hedge your portfolio.

As a substitute to publicly traded alternatives, consider owning physical property instead. Here are a few alternatives to alternatives.

Vacation home. A vacation home can become a valuable asset for you and your family. It will give you growth with an inflation hedge. Of course, it all depends on where your second home is located. A second home in Laguna Beach, Estes Park, or Nantucket will fare much better than a home located in, say, Dalhart, TX. According to CNBC, home prices have returned 5.8% per year since 1968. They also said a vacation home will cost about 20% more when compared to buying a primary home.[1]

Watches. Rolex, Cartier, or Patek Philippe are top brands. A classic time piece will cost you plenty but the long-term value may be worth the investment. A Rolex Submariner has

---

[1] http://www.cnbc.com/2015/04/17/the-time-to-invest-in-a-second-home-is-now.html, Shelly Schwartz, April 17, 2015.

averaged about a 7% annual return from 1957 to 2015.[2] A timely time piece will also look good on your wrist.

Classic cars. Buying a vintage Porsche, Ferrari, or Lamborghini can keep you ahead of the pack when driving on the road or impressing the valet. A 1955 Mercedes-Benz 300 SL sold for $1.34 million in 2015.[3]

Wine. A wine collection can pour dividends into your portfolio. There are many advantages to owning a quality wine collection, the least of which is you can drink your profits. A case of Caymus Cabernet will cost you about $2,160.

Art. Who wouldn't want to own a Warhol, Van Gogh, or Picasso? If you're going to buy art, make sure you like it, because you'll have to look at it for a long time. Most cities host art fairs where local artists are featured; this can be your entry into acquiring fashionable art. Herb and Dorothy Vogel started collecting art in the early 1960s as a young couple. They never earned more than $23,000 per year but collected thousands of pieces of art, which one curator valued as "priceless."[4]

---

[2] http://www.businessinsider.com/how-and-why-rolex-prices-have-increased-2014-12, David Bredan, January 1, 2015.
[3] https://www.bloomberg.com/news/articles/2015-12-24/vintage-porsches-are-rising-as-the-next-blue-chip-classic-cars, Hannah Elliott, December 24, 2015.
[4] http://mentalfloss.com/article/48844/how-working-class-couple-amassed-priceless-art-collection, Jed Lipinski, accessed May 24, 2017.

Timber. Buying timber land will help your portfolio grow. Timber has been a solid (wood) long term investment. I'd recommend hiring a land manager if you're a city dweller. The land manager will take care of your property and give you advice on the best time to cut your timber.

Coins. Gold and silver coins are an easy entry into the physical world of alternative investments. You can buy them online at https://www.usmint.gov/.

Beanie Babies. Just kidding.

As you construct your alternative portfolio, remember it costs money to store and own some of these investments. They aren't liquid either. If you need cash quickly, you may have trouble selling them. These investments can also be an ideal way for you to pass on your assets to the next generation. Would you rather inherit a publicly traded REIT or a beach house in Maui?

Happy collecting!

…for wisdom is more precious than rubies, and nothing you desire can compare with her. ~ Proverbs 8:11

May 23, 2017

Dow Jones = 20,937.91

109 A Letter to My Know-It-All Younger Self

At the ripe age of 22 I launched my career in the financial services industry and was set to become a master of the universe. I first worked for a major bank and then a leading Wall Street firm. After 30 years in the industry, I now realize I didn't know everything during my early days. Reflecting on my career, here are a few things I wish I'd have done differently in my early 20s.

Save more. I wish I had deposited money in a savings account or money market fund for emergencies or opportunities. This would've allowed me to stay out of debt and avoid hefty credit card charges.

Contribute more. My 401(k) plan was Greek to me and I had no idea what my options were. Even though I was in the industry I didn't know what I was doing with my own money. My employer and colleagues couldn't or wouldn't give me advice for one reason or another. I wish I'd maxed out my retirement contribution and diversified my assets.

Invest more. I should've set up a monthly investment account to buy stocks. One of my first meetings with a prospect was a friend of mine. In 1990, I recommended he invest $50 per month in the Investment Company of America mutual fund (AIVSX). A $50 monthly investment from 1990 until today is now worth $62,100. He didn't invest because he was afraid of stocks; I didn't do it because I didn't have any money.

Spend less. A dollar here and a dollar there and soon we're talking about real money. While working I'd spend $5 for breakfast and $10 for lunch. $15 might not sound like much but at the end of the year it's $3,600! Investing $3,600 per year at 7% will grow to $340,000 over 30 years.

Charge less. It's easy to start using a credit card but it's hard to stop. As a young buck, I'd spend money I didn't have, and this put me in debt. The interest rate on my credit card debt was more than 20%. If you pay the minimum payment on your credit card balance each month, you'll never pay it off – never!

Learn more. A basic understanding of finance is necessary for survival. Understanding cash flows, debt payments and the time value of money are critical to your long term financial success. Take a class, read a book, watch a video or talk to an advisor about financial literacy.

Give more. I didn't have any money when I started my finance career. Despite my lack of wealth, I could always find someone with less money. My first job was in downtown San Diego and I parked a long way from the office. I passed several homeless people on my walk to office. I had zero, but they had less than zero. I wish I had dug deep in my young pockets to help those in need.

Eat better. Habits start early so focus on eating well. Your body is a temple and should be treated with respect. Doing so will help your body age gracefully.

Run more. Not really. I ran all the time and I don't think I could've logged any more miles than I did in my youth.

Don't let anyone look down on you because you are young, but set an example for the believers in speech, in conduct, in love, in faith and in purity. ~ 1 Timothy 4:12.

May 25, 2017

Dow Jones = 21,082.94

110 What Will You Do in Retirement?

Today you're working. Tomorrow you're retired. After 18 years of schooling and 40 years of working, it's now time for retirement. For the first time in your life you don't need to set your alarm clock for a Monday morning meeting.

A question I'm often asked is, "What will I do in retirement?" Few people have a strategy for retirement. In fact, only 22% of individuals feel confident about their retirement according to the *Chicago Tribune*.[1]

Retirement has two sides: financial and emotional. The financial equation is easier to deal with. A financial planner will give you an accurate estimate of how much income you'll receive based on your current level of assets. The emotional side of retirement, however, is more challenging and difficult to quantify. Individuals aren't likely to retire until their emotional house is in order, regardless of their financial situation.

What will you do in retirement? Here are a few suggestions to help you with the emotional side.

Give. Suggesting that you give your money away in retirement hardly makes economic sense. Retirees want to know how much money they'll receive; not how much they'll give.

---

[1] http://www.chicagotribune.com/business/yourmoney/ct-marksjarvis-0422-biz-20150421-column.html, Gail Marksjarvis, April 22, 2015.

Individuals who can afford to retire and live off their savings should be able to donate some of their money. A giving or charitable strategy will help define the who, what, when, and where for your donations. Giving money away can also make you happier and healthier, according to a 2015 research report.[2] As a child you probably were told it's much better to give than receive, but you didn't believe it until you were older. Giving is advantageous to all parties.

Volunteer. Giving and volunteering are close cousins, if not siblings. Most people will tell you they're busier in retirement than they were during their working years. Non-profits are constantly looking for help. A quick Google search for non-profits in Austin, TX produced over 825,000 results. Volunteering your time will help fill your day with meaningful activity while doing good for others. Your local church, school district, or Chamber of Commerce can point you in the right direction and lead you to several serving opportunities. Joining Rotary or Kiwanis will also give you instant access to serving opportunities.

Mentor. You'll retire with a wealth of knowledge, and it would be a terrible thing to waste. Helping a student with homework or reading will bear much fruit and can change their life trajectory. Mentoring a new business, startup, or incubator can be beneficial to the young owner and help her avoid several mistakes. Your knowledge is invaluable and the lessons

---

[2] http://nypost.com/2015/09/03/people-who-donate-to-charity-are-much-happier-and-healthier/, Reuters, September 3, 2015.

you pass on to the younger generation won't soon be forgotten.

Work. Work? Who wants to work in retirement? I want to work in a fly fishing shop or outdoor adventure store. If I'm able to work in a fly fishing shop in Colorado during retirement I wouldn't consider it work. What hobbies do you have? Can you convert your hobby into employment? If you like gardening, work in a nursery. If you're an artist, work in an art store. Seasonal work may be another opportunity for you during your golden years. Working at a ski resort in the winter and a beach resort in the summer may be your ticket. Working part or full-time in retirement will also help with your finances. The longer you defer your withdrawals from your investment accounts, the more money you'll have as you mosey through retirement.

School. First work and now school? What the heck? Most universities will allow retirees to audit a class or two. Did you miss taking quantum physics as an undergrad? You now can go back to school and devote yourself to a subject of your choosing. Your local university or junior college offer hundreds of courses, giving you the opportunity to study almost anything.

Hobbies. Do you have a hobby you can convert to cash? Do you have paintings or pottery to sell? Since you're not working 9 to 5 you can allocate more time to hone your hobby or craft. What if you don't have hobbies? Retirement is an ideal time to study the guitar or learn to scuba dive.

Travel. Distant lands are calling. Travelling by land, sea, or air is good for the soul. In addition to seeing our big blue planet, you'll experience different cultures and meet amazing people. A trip to New Zealand, China, Greece, or Peru will expand your horizons. Local travel is also captivating. Visiting the National Parks is breathtaking. A hike through Yellowstone or Yosemite will leave you speechless. Sailing the seven seas will allow you to discover two-thirds of our earth. It's also possible to turn your travel into extended stays. How would you like to live in Sardinia for a few months?

Fitness. If you take care of your body, it will take care of you. Yoga, walking, swimming, cycling, or lifting weights are low-impact activities that provide numerous benefits. Regular exercise can improve sleep and reduce your risk of diabetes and heart disease.[3] 20 to 30 minutes a day is all you need to maintain or improve your health.

Fish. Fishing for trout with a Purple Haze Parachute fly while floating on the Bitterroot may be in your future. Fishing, of course, is a popular retirement hobby. Most people live near a pond, stream, river, or ocean so finding fishable water should be easy. Fishing can also be a lifelong sport enjoyable for the entire family.

Golf. Golf may be the ultimate retirement prize. A worker will endure 40 years of employment, so he can spend the rest of his life golfing. Florida, Arizona, and other sunbelt states are

---

[3] https://www.mindbodygreen.com/0-29265/does-exercise-help-reverse-the-effects-of-aging.html, Leigh Weingus, May 20, 2017.

meccas for retirees. If you're going to spend the rest of your life on the golf course, make sure you dip yourself in sunscreen regularly.

Nothing. Of course, doing nothing is an option. You may want to sit on the couch all day and watch TV. But I doubt it. Retirement is an exciting time, so I'd encourage you to get off the couch and enjoy it.

Your golden years will be the best years of your life. The ability to do what you want, when you want is highly satisfying. Your retirement will give you a chance to live life on your terms. It can be a life of leisure, but I'd encourage you to use your resources (physical, spiritual, and financial) to help others and yourself!

Happy Retirement!

Men do not quit playing because they grow old; they grow old because they quit playing. ~ Oliver Wendell Holmes

June 2, 2017

Dow Jones = 21,206.28

111 Are You Outperforming the Market?

The Standard & Poor's 500 Index is soaring, rising over 17% this year! Money managers, mutual funds, institutions, pension plans, endowments are all under pressure to beat the stock market. A money manager who outperforms this index is a hero while one who underperforms is a goat. Chasing short-term index returns might be good for the professional, but not for the individual.

The S&P 500 Index is an unmanaged basket of 500 stocks and doesn't assess fees. A money manager charges a fee, deducted from your gross return. A money manager who's up 17% and charges a 1% fee will see a client's return drop to 16%. Because of the 1% fee, the money manager is underperforming the index.

Let's look at some history before you sell your diversified portfolio and invest it all in a S&P 500 Index fund. From 2000 to 2010 the S&P 500 lost 9.1%. A $10,000 investment in January of 2000 was worth $9,090 by the end of the decade. You lost during the "lost" decade.

Do you need to outperform the stock market? It'd be nice to beat the market every year, but it's not crucial to achieving your financial goals. The ultimate index to follow is your own. A financial plan will give you the best metrics to track. It's more important to achieve your financial goals than it is to outperform the stock market.

Let's look at a few examples.

Your goal is to retire with $1 million so you can live comfortably for the rest of your life. After completing your financial plan, you realize your assets are worth $2 million. This is more than enough money to allow you to retire in style. In this scenario, you need to preserve assets, not outperform the stock market. A mix of cash, bonds and a few stocks will help you do just this.

Your goal is to retire with $1 million. Your current assets are $250,000. If you save $10,000 per year for 20 years, you'll achieve your goal with a 5% return. The stock market has averaged 7.35% for the past 20 years.[1] If you achieved your million-dollar goal, would you be upset if you didn't outperform the stock market?

You need $50,000 in annual income to maintain your lifestyle. If your portfolio generates $60,000 per year in income, your goal should be to maintain the income and not outperform the stock market. In this case you'll need a portfolio of bonds and dividend paying stocks.

Investors have two primary fears according to a study conducted by Dimensional Fund Advisors. The first is not having enough money for a comfortable retirement and the second is a significant drop in the stock market.[2] If you avoided

---

[1] Morningstar Office Hypothetical Tool.
[2] 2017 Dimensional Fund Advisor Investor Feedback Survey.

these two pitfalls, does it matter if you didn't outperform the stock market?

Focus on your goals and not the stock market. A diversified portfolio of stocks, bonds and cash will treat you well over your lifetime. Stay diversified my friends!

Everyone has the brainpower to follow the stock market. If you made it through fifth-grade math, you can do it. ~ Peter Lynch

June 6, 2017

Dow Jones = 21,136.23

112 Fishing from My Driveway

A boat resting on a driveway is safe from the wrath of Neptune. It can sit peacefully on concrete, protected from waves, tides, and rocks. However, a boat isn't made to sit idle on a driveway; it's made to be on the water. Similarly, fishing from a driveway doesn't work either. The boat and the fisherman need to be on the water.

A boat on the water is exposed to more risk, as is the fisherman. Risks increase the farther the boat travels from shore. Waves get bigger, wind howls harder, but the payoff is better.

Investing also carries many levels of risk and safety. If you're looking for total safety, you can invest in a certificate of deposit or U.S. Treasury Bill. They'll guarantee you a rate of return if you hold them to maturity. They'll also guarantee you a low rate of return, since both yield about 1%. These may work in the short term, but they don't hold water as long-term investments.

To create wealth, an investor needs to have exposure to risk assets like stocks. Their prices bob up and down like a boat on the water, but if held for the long term they'll treat you well. In the short term, stocks rise and fall to much fanfare. When they fall, the media will want to know if this is the beginning of the end. It may feel like the end of times if you've lived through the corrections of 1987, 2000, or 2008. Despite the previous storms, the stock market recovered and sailed to all-time highs. Historically, stocks have averaged a 10% annual return despite all the drops.

Set a course for adventure and invest to achieve your goals. Diversify your assets across stocks, bonds, and cash so you can keep your portfolio afloat!

A ship in harbor is safe – but that is not what ships are built for. ~ John A. Shedd

June 10, 2017

Dow Jones = 21,271.97

113 Worst Crash Ever?

Jim Rogers is a legendary investor and prolific author. In a recent interview with Business Insider, Mr. Rogers called for the worst correction ever.[1] In fact, Mr. Rogers has made similar predictions for the past six years.[2]

Worst ever? The Dow Jones Industrial Average closed at 21,235 on June 12, 2017. A correction of 85% would send the index to 3,185, a level not seen since December 1991.

The U.S. stock market has suffered some doozies over the years. Notable corrections occurred in 1907, 1973, 1974, 1987, 2000, and 2008. On October 19, 1987 it fell 22.5%. During the Great Recession of 2008, it dropped 37%. The Great Depression lasted 10 years and it's considered the worst (economic) time in our country's history, as the market fell 85% from 1929 to 1932. Despite these thunderous corrections, stocks have always recovered.

When I started my investment career in 1989 my grandfather asked if I'd read *The Great Depression of 1990* by Dr. Ravi Batra. I told him I hadn't because I didn't think it would happen. He said it's important to read several points of view to make informed decisions. I read the book. The stock market of the 90s increased 426%, reaching 10,000 before 2000. A

---

[1] http://www.businessinsider.com/jim-rogers-worst-crash-lifetime-coming-2017-6, Jacqui Frank and Kara Chin, June 9, 2017.
[2] http://awealthofcommonsense.com/2017/06/bulls-bears-charlatans/, Ben Carlson, June 11, 2017.

$10,000 investment in the Vanguard S&P 500 Index Fund (VFINX) on January 1, 1990 was worth $52,668 by December 31, 1999 averaging 18.07% per year.[3]

We also must be leery of overly optimistic forecasts. Harry S. Dent, Jr., author of *The Roaring 2000's: Building the Wealth and Lifestyle You Deserve in the Greatest Boom in History*, projected that the Dow Jones would reach 35,000 by 2008. It closed at 8,776. A $10,000 investment in the Vanguard S&P 500 Index Fund (VFINX) on January 1, 2000 was worth $10,361 by December 31, 2010 generating a return of .32% per year.[4]

It's not wise to invest based on conjecture. However, if you're concerned about the worst correction ever here are a few steps you can employ to protect your assets.

- **Avoid excessive leverage and debt.** Your total debt payments should be less than 38% of gross income. If you must use margin in your investment account, limit it to 10% of your account balance.
- **Keep a cash reserve.** Most advisors recommend keeping three to six months of expenses in a cash account.
- **Invest in Treasury Bonds.** U.S. Treasury investments will perform well during times of calamity. They're inversely related to stocks and

---

[3] Morningstar Office Hypothetical Tool.
[4] Ibid.

if stocks fall, treasuries rise. During the correction of 2008, U.S. Treasury Bonds rose 25.9%.
- **Rebalance your account.** A portfolio of stocks, bonds, and cash will fluctuate with market conditions. Rebalancing once or twice per year will return your account to its original allocation and reduce your portfolio risk.
- **Diversify.** Diversify your holdings across stocks, bonds, and cash. Your stock holdings should be allocated across large, small, and international companies.
- **Avoid concentration.** Individual stock positions comprising more than 10% of your account balance should be trimmed to 3% to 5%. Reducing your dependence on one or two stocks will benefit you during a market meltdown.

Will Mr. Rogers' prediction come true? I hope not. It's difficult to make investment decisions based on predictions, forecasts or opinions because they rarely come true. Invest according to your financial plan. A plan built on your hopes, dreams and fears will treat you well in good times and bad.

Tomorrow, tomorrow, for I know not when tomorrow will be. ~ Abigail Adams

A View from the Perch

June 12, 2017

Dow Jones = 21,235.66

114   Wonder Woman

Wonder Woman is crushing the summer box office competition. It has grossed $438.5 million so far and shows no sign of slowing down.

Wonder Woman was established by DC Comics in October of 1941 as a heroine from the Amazon and she's part of the Justice League with Batman, Superman, and Aquaman. She's been described as a feminist icon promoting peace while fighting evil.[1]

As the father of a daughter, I read books to her at an early age highlighting strong women like Amelia Earhart, Rosa Parks, Mary, Sacagawea, Mother Teresa, Margaret Mead, Helen Keller, and many more. It was important to me for her to see women of courage in trailblazing roles. She's a trailblazer herself, and she's currently working with refugees on the other side of the world.

Women are also Wonder Women when it comes to investing. Women investors have outperformed men over the past few years. Men tend to trade more often than women, a problem because of the added costs and underperformance by trying

---

[1] http://www.dccomics.com/characters/wonder-woman, website accessed June 20, 2017.

to time the market. Women, on the other hand, tend to be buy and hold investors.[2]

Women need to take charge of their planning and investments because they tend to outlive men. According to one study, 90% of women will handle money on their own due to marrying later, getting divorced and living longer than men.[3] A woman aged 65 today can expect to live to age 86.6, while men will live to 84.3.[4]

How can you lasso more financial and investment knowledge?

- **Read.** Reading books, websites, or newsletters will increase your investment acumen. Several books and websites help women investors. Here are a few I'd suggest: *Smart Women Finish Rich,* by David Bach; *Smart Women Love Money,* by Alice Finn; *The Only Investment Guide You'll Ever Need,* by Andrew Tobias.
- **Ask.** If you don't know, ask! If you're working with an advisor, make sure you understand what you own and the fees you're paying. It's your money and financial welfare, so don't be afraid to ask tough questions. If your advisor isn't

---

[2] http://money.cnn.com/2017/03/08/investing/women-better-investors-than-men/index.html, Heather Long, March 8, 2017.
[3] Ibid.
[4] https://www.ssa.gov/planners/lifeexpectancy.html, accessed June 20, 2017.

willing to answer your questions, it's time to get a new one.

- **Watch.** Webinars are valuable educational tools. A Google search can identify companies that provide financial webinars. You can watch a webinar when it's convenient for your schedule – a tremendous benefit.
- **Plan.** A good plan today is better than a perfect plan tomorrow. It will guide you towards your financial goals. A financial plan will also help you avoid pitfalls, traps, and scams. If you know where you're going, you're more likely to get there!
- **Save.** It's important to establish multiple channels for saving and investing. Investors should have, at a minimum, these accounts: savings, investment, and retirement. They can be automated to help you stay committed to your plan.
- **Beware.** Be on guard for sales promotions and investment scams promising you eye-popping returns. If it sounds too good to be true, it probably is! You can also check your broker or advisor on public websites like the SEC Investment Advisor Public Disclosure (IAPD) site, FINRA Broker Check or Brightscope. A click on an

advisor's profile will introduce you to his background and history.
- **Mentor.** Are you able to help a young lady or two get started in the world of business or investing? If you're a successful investor, can you pass on your knowledge to the next generation of wonder women? Young women are looking for strong women to help guide them financially and you may be the one to lead them on their journey.

You have the power to control your financial destiny. Take control and be brave as you set out to conquer the world of investing. I know you can do it!

I'm not afraid of storms as I am learning how to sail my ship. ~ Louisa May Alcott

June 20, 2017

Dow Jones = 21,467.14

115 Groundhog Day

Groundhog Day is a hilarious movie starring Bill Murray, Andie McDowell, and Chris Elliott. TV news reporter Phil, Bill Murray, is sent to Punxsutawney, Pennsylvania to report on the city's famous groundhog to see if winter will continue for six more weeks. Phil is stuck endlessly repeating this day and wakes up each morning to Sonny and Cher's, *I Got You Babe*. When he realizes what's happening he takes his life to extremes by overeating, jumping from buildings, sitting in the bathtub with a toaster, leaping in front of a moving truck, and hitting people in the face. No matter what he does he wakes up each morning as if nothing happened.

The stock market is like Groundhog Day. Each day reporters cover its actions, hunting for clues as to what the future may bring. If it's rising, reporters want to know if this is the beginning of a new bull market. Will it "break out" and bound forever upward or is it a trap to get individual investors to buy at a market top? Likewise, if the market is falling, the media will look for a fearmonger to report on the coming end times. The market is falling, so we must be standing on the precipice about to plunge into the abyss.

CNBC parades an army of market analysts, fund managers, experts, academics, gurus, and other fortune tellers to try to explain each tick. Guests get about 30 seconds to explain the market's movements while giving the viewer hope they know what will happen to stocks for the next five decades. Guests usually appear as part of a panel to offer various opinions.

A View from the Perch

They battle each other, trying to prove their point while the anchor is yelling at them to stop so CNBC can pivot to another "breaking news" story.

The process repeats itself every Monday through Friday, a financial *Groundhog Day*. Each day the market will rise and fall. Does it matter what happens to the daily movements of your stocks? No, because, in the end the stock market always wins. A recent chart and article posted by Market Watch highlighted the history of the Dow Jones Industrial Average from 1896 to 2016, 120 years of market data.[1] The chart subtitle is, "Human Innovation Always Trumps Fear."[2] Despite world wars, a depression, Black Monday, Black Tuesday, Pearl Harbor, Sputnik, the JFK assassination, and the Great Recession, the stock market has always recovered!

How can you avoid your financial Groundhog Day?

- Turn off your TV and enjoy life.
- Don't worry about daily movements in the market. Have faith in capitalism because financially sound companies win in the end.
- Focus on your short- and long-term financial goals. You can't control the stock market, but you can control your financial plan. It's more

---

[1] http://www.marketwatch.com/story/the-dows-tumultuous-120-year-history-in-one-chart-2017-03-23?link=sfmw_fb, Sue Chang, Markets Reporter, June 23, 2017.
[2] Ibid.

important to spend time refining your goals than it is to try and find the next hot stock.
- Diversify your investment holdings to reduce your portfolio risk. A well-constructed portfolio of stocks, bonds, and cash can keep you invested in good times and bad.
- Extend your investment time horizon to avoid short-term ripples in the stock market. From 1926 to 2014 there have been 70 rolling 20-year periods and the stock market has made money 100% of the time.[3]

It's easy to get sucked into the whirlpool of a financial Groundhog Day, so you must be diligent in focusing on your goals. The simple act of thinking about generational wealth will keep you moving forward towards your goals.

Turn your face to the sun and the shadows fall behind you. ~ Maori Proverb

June 24, 2017

Dow Jones = 21,394.75

---

[3] Ibbotson®SBBI® 2015 Classic Year Book, Market Results for Stocks, Bonds, Bills and Inflation 1926–2014.

116 First, Do No Harm

The Hippocratic Oath is taken by physicians and is considered the source of medical ethics.[1] It's named after Hippocrates, who lived during the 5th century B.C. A section of the modern version of the oath is, "I will remember that there is art to medicine as well as science, and that warmth, sympathy, and understanding may outweigh the surgeon's knife or the chemist's drug."[2]

What's missing from the Hippocratic Oath is the phrase, "First, do no harm." The popular saying isn't part of the oath; however, the spirit of the term remains.[3]

Can you imagine visiting a doctor who hasn't taken the Hippocratic Oath? I can't. When I visit my doctor, I assume he's taken the oath and will do no harm, especially to me. A doctor is expected to administer medical care regardless of the circumstance.

During the College World Series between LSU and Florida, Dr. Jerry Poche, father of LSU star pitcher Jared Poche, helped save the life of an elderly fan. Dr. Poche and Jimmy Roy, another parent, administered CPR until the paramedics

---

[1] https://www.nlm.nih.gov/hmd/greek/greek_oath.html, Michael North, National Library of Medicine, 2002.
[2] http://www.psychceu.com/ethics/do_no_harm.asp, 1964, Louis Lasagna, Academic Dean of the School of Medicine at Tufts University.
[3] http://guides.library.jhu.edu/c.php?g=202502&p=1335752.

arrived.[4] Dr. Poche acted swiftly to save the gentleman's life and he did no harm.

Registered Investment Advisors are under a fiduciary oath. The National Association of Personal Financial Advisors (NAPFA) fiduciary oath starts with the sentence: "Always act in good faith and with candor."[5] The fiduciary standard originated with the Investment Advisors Act of 1940, and recently the Department of Labor passed the fiduciary rule requiring all financial professionals who work with retirement plans or provide retirement planning advice to be fiduciaries.

The Certified Financial Planner Board requires members to adhere to the fiduciary standard when providing financial planning services, but this may change to include investment advice. In a sense, any individual who holds the CFP designation will be required to always act as a fiduciary.

As you look for an advisor to help you with your financial planning and investment advice, look for one who's a fiduciary and has taken the oath!

And let us not grow weary of doing good, for in due season we will reap, if we do not give up. ~ Galatians 6:9

---

[4] http://www.nola.com/lsu/index.ssf/2017/06/a_pair_of_lsu_baseball_dads_re.html, Andrew Lopez, June 27, 2017.

[5] https://www.napfa.org/mission-and-fiduciary-oath.

A View from the Perch

July 2, 2017

Dow Jones = 21,479.26

117 Are You an All-Star Investor?

The 88th Major League Baseball All-Star Game honoring the game's best players will be played Tuesday in Miami. The All-Star game has included perennial legends like Hank Aaron, Willie Mays and Stan Musial, Nolan Ryan and Cal Ripken.

We'll watch Dodger ace, Clayton Kershaw and Angels outfielder, Mike Trout along with other future Hall of Famers. Despite the talents of these players, they still must work at their craft. Miami's Suzuki Ichirio is in relentless pursuit of perfection on the baseball field. He spends hours stretching and swinging and according to C.C. Sabathia, Ichirio only takes two days off – the day after the season ends and Christmas.[1]

All-Stars have down days too. As good as these players are, they still strike out, commit errors and throw wild pitches. However, they continue to play through the dark days, knowing the odds of success are in their favor. A strong work ethic, constant practice, and a positive outlook will soon pay off.

Are you an investor all-star? Do you have what it takes to be among the all-time investor greats? I believe you do, and with a few simple tweaks to your investing routine, you can be an

---

[1] https://www.nytimes.com/2015/10/04/sports/baseball/ichiro-suzuki-aiming-at-age-50-but-first-3000-hits.html?mcubz=1, David Waldstein, October 3, 2015.

all-star. Let's look at a few ideas that can help you star in the investing game.

- **Plan.** Great managers of the game of baseball have a plan. Tommy Lasorda, Walter Alston, and Joe Torre had a plan for each game. Likewise, you too should have your own plan. A well-constructed one will help you become an all-star investor. It will help you achieve your hopes and dreams.
- **Lineup.** Casey Stengal once said, "Good pitching will always stop good hitting and vice versa." A strong lineup is tough to beat. The 1927 Yankees are considered by many to be the best baseball team of all time. Their "Murderer's Row" consisted of Earle Combs, Babe Ruth, Lou Gehrig, and Tony Lazzeri, all of whom are in the Baseball Hall of Fame. A strong lineup of low-cost, diversified index funds will keep you in the game for a long time and produce winning results.
- **Routine.** Baseball players are superstitious. Wade Boggs ate chicken before every baseball game. To increase your odds of success you should develop a routine. I recommend a dollar cost averaging and rebalancing. Dollar cost averaging means investing the same dollar

amount each month. If you participate in your company's retirement plan, you're dollar cost averaging every pay period. Following this strategy with other investments will pay big league dividends. Rebalancing your portfolio will reduce your risk and keep your original asset allocation intact. I recommend rebalancing once per year, typically in January.

- **Play.** "Progress always involves risks. You can't steal second base and keep your foot on first base," said Frederick B. Wilcox. To be an all-star investor you need to own stocks. Stocks are perpetual all-stars and have outperformed bonds and cash by a wide margin. A dollar invested in the S&P 500 in 1926 is worth $6,031 today. This same dollar invested in a one-month US Treasury Bill is worth $21![2]

- **Review.** Baseball players watch tape on opposing players and themselves for clues of how to gain an advantage. Reviewing your accounts quarterly will keep you in peak form. As you review your accounts look at winners and losers. Do you need to make any adjustments or changes? A quarterly review is an opportunity to make sure your investments are in line with your financial game plan.

---

[2] Dimensional Fund Advisors Matrix Book 2017.

- **Celebrate.** Derek Jeter's last game at Yankee Stadium was epic. The Yankees and Orioles were tied in the bottom of the ninth when Jeter came to the plate. To put a punctuation point on his stellar career he had the game winning hit and everyone in Yankee stadium erupted in applause. As you gain success as an investor take some time to enjoy the fruits of your labor.

Get your game on and become an investing all-star. I know you can do it! Your talent, combined with discipline, practice and patience will give you major league results! Batter up!

Ruth, Gehrig, DiMaggio, Mantle … Costanza?! ~ Jerry Seinfeld

July 8, 2017

Dow Jones = 21,414.33

118   Ready for a New Retirement?

Do you love new things like driving a new car off the dealer's lot? How about getting a new pair of shoes? We like getting new gifts, but how about a new retirement? Are we ready for this?

Corporations continue to scale back on pensions and benefits. In 2015, 99 companies in the Fortune 500 offered a pension plan, down from 292 in 1998, a drop of 66%.[1] Only 9% of the Fortune 100 offer full healthcare benefits, a drop from 34% in 2001.[2]

My wife's grandfather worked his entire career for a large oil company in Texas. He retired with a pension allowing him to receive a lifetime income stream for both himself and his wife. Payments from his former employer would continue for as long as one of them was living. In addition, they didn't have any out-of-pocket expenses for health and medical benefits, including drug prescriptions, as these items were covered by the company. His pension, coupled with his Social Security payments, allowed him to enjoy a substantial retirement income.

---

[1] https://www.businessinsurance.com/article/20160222/NEWS03/160229986, Jerry Geisel, February 22, 2016.
[2] http://fortune.com/2016/03/30/employer-paid-health-insurance-is-dying-off/, Lauren Lorenzetti, March 30, 2016.

Today, workers will have 10 to 15 jobs over their working career, with an average of 12.[3] A college graduate who retires at age 65 may switch jobs every three to four years. By switching jobs often, a worker won't accrue much in the way of company retirement benefits. If you join a company with a 401(k), you may have to wait a year to join and if you leave before year's end you might forfeit the employer contribution. By repeating this process over time, you'll leave a lot of money on the table.

Living longer can also cause heartache for the retiree. A long, happy retirement can be enjoyable especially if you have money. But longevity risk is making this a challenge for some. According to the Motley Fool, Social Security will cover about 40% of your retirement income and the average monthly benefit will be $1,350.[4] This means you're responsible for the other 60% of your income. According to the Social Security life expectancy tables, an individual aged 65 today will live another 19 years to 84. Will your retirement assets generate income for 19 years?

What does this mean for today's worker? We have entered a brave new world of retirement. Responsibility for retirement is now on your shoulders and you must bear the weight of

---

[3] https://www.thebalance.com/how-often-do-people-change-jobs-2060467, Alison Doyle, May 1, 2017.
[4] https://www.fool.com/retirement/2016/10/23/can-you-live-on-social-security-alone.aspx, Chuck Saletta, October 23, 2016.

making your money last a lifetime. However, you're not alone. With the right help, you can achieve financial security.

To start on your new journey, you'll need a plan. A financial and retirement plan will give you a financial target and this will be your guiding light as you journey through your working career. Your financial plan will outline the amount of money you'll need to save to achieve your goal.

But to reach your goal, you'll need to commit to it as well. I met with a friend recently who was bemoaning the fact he didn't have enough money saved for retirement. We talked about a few ideas, but he wasn't willing to commit – yet. He likes to eat out often and his Facebook page shows him on elaborate treks with his family. At some point he'll need to bear down and get serious about his financial future.

Besides creating and committing to a plan, you must save money. Contributing to your company retirement plans, IRAs, and investment accounts is paramount. Saving money today will pay dividends tomorrow. A worker who starts saving $1,000 a month at age 25 will have $6.3 million at age 65. However, her assets will only be worth $759,000 if she waits until age 45 to start saving, a drop of 87%![5] Automate your savings to accumulate assets by establishing a regular draft between your bank and your investment accounts.

---

[5] FV calculation with assets growing at 10% before taxes and fees.

You can control your spending and saving. Spending less and saving more will be a winning formula for a secure retirement, so put your plan into action today! I know you can do it!

All hard work brings a profit, but mere talk leads only to poverty. ~ Proverbs 14:23

July 13, 2017

Dow Jones = 21,553.08

119   Save It or Spend It?

Money can't buy happiness, and the Bible says the *love* of money is the root of evil. A 2015 survey by the American Psychological Association found 64% of Americans say money is a source of stress.[1] When it comes to money we have a couple of choices – save it or spend it.

Peggy has been a client of mine for over 25 years. We've enjoyed a great relationship and during our recent quarterly review of her accounts we mostly talked about her travel experiences. She has taken amazing trips during her lifetime and they've created lifelong memories. She told me a story about a trip she made with her young family to Crater Lake in Oregon. She recounted the beauty of the area, especially the brilliant blue water. She didn't recall the cost of the trip, but years later still receives joy when thinking about her experience.

Peggy and I have adopted a buy and hold strategy for her investments, owning a mix of high quality mutual funds. Every year she will withdraw money to fund her trips. We've experienced many market cycles together and, despite several stock market corrections, five U.S. presidents and annual withdrawals, her account continues to grow and support her lifestyle. She's a bold and courageous investor who's unafraid

---

[1] http://www.cnbc.com/2015/08/03/most-americans-rich-or-not-stressed-about-money-surveys.html, Shelly Schwartz, August 3, 2015.

of market drops. Her investment strategy has served her well over time.

It has been said that money can't buy happiness, but this isn't entirely true. According to a Wall Street Journal article on money and happiness, "People think that experiences are only going to provide temporary happiness, but they actually provide both more happiness and more lasting value."[2]

Here are a few tips to help you decide between saving and spending.

Take the trip. It's time to spend some money on your dream trip and cross it off your bucket list. It may be expensive and cause a dent in your net worth but when you reminisce about it years from now, you'll be glad you did. When our daughter was young, my wife and I decided to take amazing trips, so we could create incredible memories. I'm glad we spent the money because I look back on our family trips with fondness and happiness.

Do it today and don't wait for tomorrow. If you wait for the perfect time in your life or a certain level of assets, you'll never take that trip. Also, we don't know what tomorrow will bring. A former client of mine was waiting until he retired to travel the country with his wife but a month after he retired she

---

[2] https://www.wsj.com/articles/can-money-buy-happiness-heres-what-science-has-to-say-1415569538, Andrew Blackman, November 10, 2014.

passed away. Proverbs 27:1 says, "Do not boast about tomorrow, for you do not know what a day may bring."

Use your vacation days. Most employees don't take their paid vacation for fear of not getting their work done or having their employer question their dedication.[3] If your company is giving, you should be taking. It's true that your work won't get done, but I doubt your company will question your dedication.

Invest for growth and dividends. A portfolio designed for growth and income will help fund your experiences. It's also okay to spend your principal on your trips because the growth of your investments will replace what you removed from your account. If you turn on your faucet to fill up a tub with water and remove the water with a bucket, it will be replenished with the running water from the tap. Let's say you invested $100,000 in the Vanguard S&P 500 Index Fund (VFINX) on August 31, 1976 and started withdrawing 5% of your account balance every year. As of June 30, 2017, 41 years later, your original $100,000 investment is worth $855,000 and you've taken out over $883,000.[4]

Post it. Post your wonderful trip on Facebook or Instagram so your friends can see what an amazing time you're having and perhaps they'll be inspired to take trips of their own!

---

[3] http://www.marketwatch.com/story/55-of-american-workers-dont-take-all-their-paid-vacation-2016-06-15, Quentin Fottrell, May 28, 2017.
[4] Morningstar Office Hypothetical Tool as of June 30, 2017.

Take Peggy's advice and travel the world. You'll be glad you did!

The world is a book, and those who do not travel read only a page. ~ Saint Augustine

July 16, 2017

Dow Jones = 21,629.72

120 Rock on Brother!

U2 produces powerful music. I first heard their song *New Year's Day* in 1983 and was mesmerized by the band and the music. Bands like U2, ZZ Top, Aerosmith, and Rush have produced quality music for decades. The Rolling Stones have been playing together since 1962! These bands are consistent, so fans attending their concerts know what to expect. In 1987, I attended a U2 concert in San Diego and my expectations were exceeded.

Rock bands can teach us a few lessons on how to become better investors.

- **Quality.** These bands produce quality music that is still being enjoyed by generations of listeners. Construct a portfolio of high quality investments so it can sustain your account for generations. Companies with strong balance sheets and solid earnings will deliver rock star returns for your portfolio.
- **Consistency.** The long-term survival of these bands can be credited to their consistent music. They weren't one hit wonders like Dexys Midnight Runners or Haircut 100, nor did they succumb to popular fads like wearing hammer time pants. The best bands focus on what they do best. Steady, consistent returns will give you solid investment performance. So don't try to

time the market or get caught up in the latest investment fad. Pursue a buy and hold strategy by owning index funds with low fees.
- **Plan.** Successful bands just don't happen without a plan. Writing music, singing songs, and performing at concerts takes careful planning and lots of persistence. Following a financial plan will ensure that your goals and investments are working in concert to help you achieve financial success.
- **Patience.** U2 was founded in 1976, but it wasn't until their 1983 album *War* that their band achieved global fame. Patience is also required as an investor. It may take three to five years or more before your investments start to hum financially. Set your eyes on the long term and don't worry about short-term fluctuations in your account balances.
- **Balanced.** Classic bands use multiple instruments to bring us wonderful music. They don't rely on one instrument or one performer to deliver results. The balance in the band is what keeps fueling their run. The intelligent investor will use multiple investments like stocks, bonds and cash to achieve positive results. A balanced portfolio will also help smooth out your returns over time.

- **Global.** U2 was founded in Dublin, the Beatles in Liverpool, and Van Halen in Pasadena. If these bands only played in front of the home crowd, it's doubtful they would've achieved global success. To achieve global success in your portfolio you need to venture to distant lands by adding international investments to your account.

As you construct your financial opus follow the lead of the legendary bands and focus on quality, persistence, and longevity. Rock on!

Music can change the world because it can change people. ~ Bono

July 24, 2017

Dow Jones = 21,513.16

121 An Interview with Myself

Good afternoon and welcome to my interview with Bill Parrott, President and CEO of Parrott Wealth Management in Austin, Texas.

Bill, thank you for taking time out of your day to sit down with me and answer a few questions about your business.

My pleasure, Bill. I appreciate you reaching out to me and I look forward to our interview.

Great. Let's get down to it. Why did you start your own firm?

I started my own firm to offer more services like financial planning and investment management to individuals free of any conflicts. I also wanted to be a true fiduciary and put the interests of my clients first.

You've been in the investment business a long time. Why start your business now?

Well, that's a good question. I've been in the investment business for 28 years and I've worn many hats, from financial advisor to branch manager. In 2015, I turned 50 and my daughter was applying to college and I thought to myself if I don't start my own business now I never well. In addition, my previous employer was flying me all over the country to present investment workshops and meet with clients. The travel was becoming a bit much and I wanted to spend more time with my family and work with clients in my neighborhood. After you've seen one airport terminal, you've seen them all.

Excellent. Tell me about your process when working with a new client.

When I meet with a new client I try to get a good understanding of their financial situation by offering a financial plan and risk tolerance profile. In addition to the questionnaire, I spend a fair amount of time talking to them about their financial goals and dreams. The time I spend discussing their financial situation gives me a good idea of how to structure their investment accounts. I may meet with them five or six times before we decide to open a new account.

Once you set up a client account how often do they hear from you?

I offer to meet with clients quarterly to discuss their accounts and the market. The quarterly meetings are a fantastic way to check in to see if anything has changed in their lives. In addition to the quarterly meetings, I email a monthly newsletter to clients and potential clients. I'm willing to meet with anybody at any time, especially if they need help. I also make house calls!

I looked at your fee schedule and it seems awfully low. Can you tell me about your fee structure?

Ha Ha! I'm often told my fee schedule is too low, but it works for me and more importantly it works for my clients. My fee structure is simple and clear. The fee is .5% on the first $10 million in assets. My fee is about half of the industry average. In addition, I charge a flat $1,500 for a financial plan. I don't charge any other fees and I don't have any minimums.

Your fee is low! What type of investments do you offer?

In addition to my low fee, I offer low-cost investments like index funds and exchange traded funds from Dimensional Fund Advisors, Vanguard, and Blackrock. These three fund families are excellent financial partners because they don't charge a sales commission and their internal fees are extremely low. I like working with these firms because they also have a client-first mentality.

How do your clients keep up with their accounts?

T.D. Ameritrade is my custodian and clients can view their accounts 24/7 on their phone, iPad, or computer. T.D. Ameritrade will send a monthly statement to the client listing all their positions. On a quarterly basis, I send a detailed report from Morningstar highlighting their performance, fees, gains, losses, income and much more.

Do you have any employees?

I do. I have an assistant who works with me and her name is Janet Jackson.

Janet Jackson?

Yes. Janet has a great name and we've been friends for a long time. We started working together on the same day when we were hired by Dean Witter in Pasadena in 1990! She is a tremendous resource and helps with onboarding new clients and helping me with the firm paperwork.

I love your logo. Can you tell me more about it?

I've been blessed with a colorful last name and so I wanted to incorporate it in my business. I've been told you shouldn't name your business after yourself but not everybody has a cool last name like mine! Ha! Ha! I wanted a bright and colorful logo that would make people smile as well. My daughter added the pie chart to the letter "O" which is a nice touch.

Bill, thank you for your time. It sounds like you love the business and have a genuine concern for your clients. How can people get in touch with you?

You know me well! I can be reached at bill@parrottwealth.com and my website is www.parrottwealth.com.

I notice you end your blogs with a Bible verse or quote. What do you have for us today?

Here is a good one, or two, from Matthew:

Jesus replied: "Love the Lord your God with all your heart and with all your soul and with all your mind." This is the first and greatest commandment. And the second is like it: "Love your neighbor as yourself." ~ Matthew 22:36–39

A good one. Thank you!

A View from the Perch

My pleasure.

August 22, 2017

Dow Jones = 21,899.89

122 10 Ways to Improve Your 401(k) Plan!

Your 401(k) plan may be your largest asset, even larger than your home. However, it appears most individuals pay little attention to this treasured benefit. In my experience, working with 401(k) providers and companies several employees sign up for their plan without giving much thought to their contribution amount or investment choices. To increase your odds for a successful and confident retirement, take time and get advice on setting up your plan.

According to the Employee Benefits Research Institute, 18% of workers feel very confident about their ability to enjoy a comfortable retirement, a number that hasn't changed since 1993.[1] What about the remaining 82%? 82% of the working population aren't confident about the future of their retirement.

Here are few ideas to help you improve your 401(k) plan and your retirement.

Start. Don't delay in signing up for your company retirement plan. As soon as you're eligible, sign on the dotted line and start contributing. The sooner you start contributing, the larger your retirement nest egg will be.

---

[1] http://www.marketwatch.com/story/what-ive-learned-over-14-years-of-covering-the-depressing-but-crucial-topic-of-retirement-2017-09-29, Robert Powell, September 29, 2017.

Max out. You can contribute $18,000 to your plan each year. If you're 50 or older, you can contribute an extra $6,000 to your plan for a total of $24,000. Contributing $18,000 for 45 years at 7% will grow to $5.1 million by the time you're ready to retire.

Contribute. If you can't afford to max out your contribution, contribute 10% of your income. If you can't contribute 10%, then match your company match. If your company matches 4%, your contribution should be 4%. If you earn $50,000 per year, your 10% contribution will be $5,000. Contributing $5,000 to your plan for 45 years growing at 7% will be worth $1.4 million at your retirement.

Escalate. Your plan may include an auto-escalation button allowing you to increase your contribution percentage annually. For example, if you start contributing 4%, you can sign up for an annual 1% increase forever or until it reaches a pre-determined percentage. Your contribution this year will be 4% and next year it will increase to 5% and so on.

Diversify. Your plan probably has six to seven investment categories like large, small, and international companies along with alternative investments and bonds or cash. To be successful, you'll need to own more growth investments than safe ones. A 70%/30% allocation might look like this: 35% large companies, 10% small companies, 20% international companies, 5% alternative investments and 30% bonds. You don't need to allocate any money to cash unless you're retiring this year.

Be aggressive. Your working career may span 45 years or more so take advantage of the long-term trend of the stock market. Also, you'll be contributing to your 401(k) every two weeks, giving you the opportunity to buy stocks when they're up, down, or sideways. I once worked with a group of anesthesiologists in Austin and, not surprisingly, the doctors with the most aggressive investment profile had the largest account balances. Some of the senior doctors I worked with had invested 100% of their 401(k) balance in stocks when they were young, and they never changed their asset allocation. This resulted in large nest eggs.

Rebalance. Rebalancing your 401(k) once per year will keep your desired risk level in check. The best time to rebalance your plan is in January. This will allow the dividends, interest payments, and capital gains to be contributed to your plan from the previous year. Your plan might have an automatic rebalancing button you can turn on when you log in to your plan.

Align. It's important for your contributions, asset allocation, and rebalancing targets to be aligned. For example, if you're contributing 35% to large companies, your asset allocation and rebalancing options should also be set to 35%.

Stay. In the gig economy workers are changing jobs every two to three years and, as a result, they may be hurting their retirement plan. By moving from one company to the next, you're leaving valuable dollars on the table and missing a company match or two. In addition, when you join a new company you may miss an enrollment window, keeping you out of your new company plan for six months to a year. These small misses will have major implications on your retirement. If you're employed by a good company with a solid retirement plan, then stay the course and let your retirement benefits accrue for you and your family.

Review. You should review your plan and investment choices once per year. You don't need to spend much more time on your plan beyond your annual review. In fact, the less you touch your plan the better.

Treat your treasured asset with respect by contributing what you can afford, investing for growth and rebalancing annually. Allocating time and resources to your plan will allow you to have a much more bountiful retirement.

You can be young without money, but you can't be old without it. ~ Tennessee Williams

September 30, 2017

Dow Jones = 22,405.09

123   I'm Proud of You!

Well done! Bravo! I'm proud of you for staying invested in the stock market for the entire year. Despite political unrest, nuclear threats, fires, floods, and hurricanes, you didn't waiver. Your resilience has paid off handsomely and you've been rewarded with outsized gains.

It was a stellar year for investors. The Dow Jones Industrial Average returned 25.5% and the S&P 500, 19.8%. A balanced portfolio consisting of 60% stocks and 40% bonds produced a one-year gain of 14.8%.

Here are some highs (and lows) that made 2017 special:

- Donald J. Trump was inaugurated as the 45th president of the United States.
- North Korea tested multiple missiles.
- 1 million women marched on Washington D.C. for women's rights.
- *Star Wars: The Last Jedi, Beauty and the Beast*, and *Wonder Woman* dominated the box office.
- The U.K. filed Article 50 to leave the European Union.
- SpaceX launched over a dozen rockets.
- The total solar eclipse mesmerized viewers.
- Hurricane Harvey destroyed a large swath of Houston, Texas.

- Hurricane Irma terrorized the Caribbean, doing the most harm to Puerto Rico.
- The Houston Astros won their first ever World Series, beating the Dodgers in 7 games.
- The New England Patriots won the Super Bowl – again.
- The California Wildfires torched over 1 million acres.
- The horrific, senseless tragedy in Las Vegas took the life of 58 souls.
- Leonardo da Vinci's painting, *Salvator Mundi*, sold for $450 million.
- The International Olympic Committee banned Russia from the 2018 Winter Olympics.
- The Federal Reserve raised its benchmark interest rate.
- Congress passed the Tax Cuts and Jobs Act.
- Bitcoin is at the center of the crypto currency craze.
- Prince Harry is engaged.
- Always Dreaming won the Kentucky Derby.

As we move towards 2018, I'd encourage you to follow your financial plan and stay invested. One of the best ways to create long-term wealth is to own quality stocks from around the world. A balanced portfolio of low-cost mutual funds will give you the exposure you need to participate in the upward trend of the stock market. Furthermore, a buy and hold strategy will allow you to enjoy the market's historical returns.

Give yourself a pat on the back and celebrate your good year! Well done! Bravo! Encore!

The more you praise and celebrate your life, the more there is in life to celebrate. ~ Oprah Winfrey

December 29, 2017

Dow Jones = 24,719.22

124 Will Stocks Rise Forever?

Voyager 1 was launched on September 5, 1977 by Jet Propulsion Laboratory (JPL) and it's currently 13 billion miles from Earth travelling at a speed of 38,000 miles per hour.[1] It's the only man-made object in interstellar space and it recently fired up its boosters after 37 years.[2] The original mission for Voyager was to study Jupiter and Saturn but now it appears it will travel through space forever.

The Dow Jones Industrial Average passed through 26,000 today and shows no sign of slowing down. Is it possible we've entered a new galaxy for stocks where they always rise and never fall? It feels like it, but I doubt it. Since March 9, 2009, the Dow Jones has risen 19,557 points or 303%.

How does this run compare to previous bull markets? The longest running bull market occurred during the 50s and 60s when the Dow rose for 15 years and soared 936%. After the Great Depression, it rose for 14 years and gained 815%. In the 80s and 90s there were two bull markets both lasting 13 years. The 80s market rose 845% and the 90s, 816%.[3] It appears this current bull market has more fuel in the tank.

---

[1] https://voyager.jpl.nasa.gov/.
[2] https://voyager.jpl.nasa.gov/news/details.php?article_id=108.
[3] https://www.ftportfolios.com/Common/ContentFileLoader.aspx?ContentGUID=4ecfa978-d0bb-4924-92c8-628ff9bfe12d, accessed January 16, 2018.

Of course, stocks can't rise forever without a correction and gravity will eventually take over. A bull market is always followed by a bear market. Since 1930 there have been eight significant corrections with the worst one occurring during the Great Depression when stocks fell 85%. The 2000 Tech Wreck brought the market down 44%, and during the Great Recession it fell 50%.[4]

What can you do now as the market continues to rocket higher? Here are four suggestions.

- Your financial plan is your command module. It controls your asset allocation and investment selection based on your financial goals. It will help guide your decisions through bull and bear markets.
- If you're invested with a diversified portfolio, keep your trajectory because a buy and hold strategy is difficult to beat. Since 1926 the stock market has averaged a 10% annual return.
- If you've missed this bull run and you hold a large cash position, then start to buy stocks and bonds. This can be done with a lump-sum purchase or through dollar-cost averaging.
- You can wait for the market to correct and buy the dip. It takes fortitude to buy stocks when

---

[4] Ibid.

others are selling, but this is when you'll get the best prices. Warren Buffett said, "Be greedy when others are fearful."

The market's rise has been meteoric, and we can start to see airglow, but it doesn't mean we're going to fall into a black hole. There's no radar system to warn us of a correction, so invest according to your plan and adjust it as needed.

Houston, Tranquility Base here. The Eagle has landed.* ~ *Neil A. Armstrong

January 16, 2018

Dow Jones = 25,792.86

125 Can Stocks Go to Zero?

The recent rout in stocks has been unnerving; the rate of decline has been swift and violent. In less than two weeks the Dow Jones has fallen more than 9%. Market corrections aren't fun, but they're normal. Up markets follow down markets and vice versa just as spring follows winter. Stocks can't go to zero and snow eventually melts.

Since 2008 the stock market has climbed more than 106%. However, this rise hasn't been without disruption. Over the past 10 years, there have been five double digit percentage declines, or about one every two years. In 2008 it plunged 50%, it dropped 18% in 2011, it fell 16% in 2015, and it declined 13% in 2016. This year it has fallen 9%. Despite these drops, a buy and hold investor still managed to generate an average annual return of 7.5%. A $100,000 investment 10 years ago is now worth $206,100.

Dating back to 1928, the stock market has finished a year in negative territory 24 times, or one in every four years. Throughout the past 90 years it has averaged an annual return of 9.6%.

Paradoxically, when stocks fall they become safer. Valuations become cheaper and dividend yields rise, giving you an opportunity to buy at attractive prices.

An investor who purchased the Dimensional Funds Core Equity 1 mutual fund (DFEOX) on October 1, 2007 enjoyed a gain of 135%. A $100,000 investment grew to $235,000. If she waited until March of 2009, after the market had fallen 50%, her initial investment would be worth $484,000, a gain of 384%.[1]

What can you do to protect your assets? Here are a few suggestions.

Follow your financial plan. Your plan should give you peace during a market decline because your investments will be synchronized to your goals. It's your financial GPS.

Diversify your assets. Diversification is the only free lunch on Wall Street. A diversified portfolio allows you to own securities from around the world. In addition, you can reduce your risk by adding cash, bonds, and alternative investments to your portfolio.

Invest in cash. If your time horizon is three years or less, move some money to a cash account, CD, or T-Bill. Do you have to pay tuition? Buy a home? Pay off your mortgage? Take a trip? Buy a car? If so, invest this money in a secure instrument that won't lose value if stocks fall.

Buy the dip. If your time horizon is more than five years, buy the dip when the market falls. The market in the short term is unpredictable but over time it has risen.

---

[1] Morningstar Hypothetical Tool, returns through January 2018.

Buy funds. A portfolio of mutual funds will give you more diversification than one that only invests in common stocks. A mutual fund will allow you to own thousands of securities.

Dollar cost average. Set up an automatic investment plan that allows you to buy stocks monthly. Automating this process will remove your emotions from your investment decisions.

Focus on the percentage not the point. A 500-point drop in 1987 was 22%, today it's 2%.

Think long term. There are about 72,000 individuals who are older than 100 living in the United States. This number could rise to 1 million by 2050.[2] A person who retires at 65 could spend 35 years or more in retirement!

Turn off your media outlets. Pundits, reporters, and commentators like to stir the pot during a market retreat. They dramatize the information for millions, but they know nothing about your specific situation.

The stock market has been fluctuating for centuries, and it will probably continue to do so long after we're gone. Focus on your goals, diversify your assets, think long-term and good things should happen.

---

[2] http://www.thecentenarian.co.uk/how-many-people-live-to-hundred-across-the-globe.html, Steven Goodman, January 17, 2018.

A View from the Perch

Bull markets are born on pessimism, grow on skepticism, mature on optimism, and die on euphoria. ~ *Sir John Templeton*

February 1, 2018

Dow Jones = 26,186.71

126 More, More, More!

Retirement is a joyous occasion and a time for celebration. After years of toil, you've earned the right to enjoy the fruits of your labor. You can travel the world, run on an uninhabited beach, read lengthy novels, watch movies, or volunteer your time. Regardless of your goals it will take money to finance your dreams.

A person retiring today at age 65 may spend 35 years in retirement. How much money will she need to fund this stage of her life? The answer is more, as in more than you think. With a few key inputs like expenses or income, it's possible to calculate how much money she'll need to fund her current lifestyle. For example, if her annual expenses are $100,000 per year, then she'll need at least $2.5 million in assets.

As you approach retirement, if not sooner, I recommend calculating your annual expenses, so you can determine the amount of assets you'll need to support your lifestyle. A budget worksheet can help you determine your monthly and annual expenses. Here's a link to a budget worksheet: https://www.consumer.gov/content/make-budget-worksheet.

If the inputs are known, why should we plan for more income? Two reasons: inflation and unexpected expenses. Inflation has averaged 3% since 1926. The value of a dollar in 1926 is only worth 7 cents today. Inflation will annihilate your cash and bond investments over time by reducing their purchasing power. However, you can offset this decline by owning stocks. Stocks have generated a real-return (net of inflation) of 6.8% since 1802.[1] Stocks will allow you to maintain your purchasing power in retirement.

The second reason you'll need more money is because of unexpected expenses like a new roof, air-conditioning unit, or car. In addition, the odds of incurring medical expenses increase as you age, unfortunately. Unexpected expenses can also come from benevolent decisions like charitable donations or gifts to loved ones.

How can you insulate yourself so you can enjoy a fruitful retirement? Here are a few ideas and suggestions.

Save more. The more money you save today, the more you'll have tomorrow. Saving an extra $500 per month will put an additional $260,000 in your pocket over 20 years.

Reduce your expenses. After reviewing your expenses, are there items in your budget you can reduce or eliminate? Lowering your expenses will give you some margin in retirement if you're confronted with unexpected expenses.

Pay off debt. Reduce your debt obligations before you enter retirement. This will lower your expenses and increase your cash flow at a time when you need it most. If you have money in the bank, use it to pay off your debt obligations.

---

[1] *Stocks for the Long Run*, Jeremy Siegel, updated.

Create a new expense category. If you follow a budget, create a line item for unexpected expenses. I've added a "black swan" category on my spread sheet for items out of my control. Why a black swan? A black swan is a rare, and often unexpected, sight. The amount of this category should be 1% to 2% of your total expenses. For example, if your expenses are $100,000 per year, then 1% to 2% of this amount is $1,000 to $2,000. This figure is now part of your budget and will help you deal with unexpected expenses.

Defer Social Security. You'll be eligible to receive Social Security at age 62, but for every year you defer your benefit, you'll get an 8% raise. A monthly benefit of $1,500 at 62 could rise to $2,776 at 70, an increase of 85%.

Retirement is a wonderful time, I'm told, which probably is the reason it's called the Golden Years. A proper retirement plan can help keep your golden years free of tarnish!

The question isn't at what age I want to retire, it's at what income. ~ George Foreman

February 6, 2018

Dow Jones = 24,912.77

127 How to Generate (More) Income in Retirement

Do you want more income for your golden years? With low interest rates and reduced pensions retirees have been on a journey to find alternative sources of income. Retirees have historically relied on Social Security benefits, pension payments, or investment income to meet their needs during retirement. These traditional income streams have been the source of survival for many.

The asset level of a retiree determines how much income she could receive. For example, if an individual retired with $1 million, she could expect to receive about $40,000 in annual income. She'd collect this investment income, along with Social Security, to meet her living needs. In years past these two items may have been her only choices.

However, through the Sharing Economy she can now generate multiple streams of income on her terms from items she already owns or possesses. She can now free herself from low-yielding bank CDs and expensive insurance products.

Another benefit to the Sharing Economy is owning fewer assets. A car is a major expense. In addition to monthly payments, there's insurance, storage, and maintenance. These expenses will take a big chunk out of her monthly income, but thanks to Uber she doesn't need to own a car.

Here's a list of companies you can tap into today to start generating more income for your retirement.

Uber and Lyft. If you own a car and have some free time, you can drive for Uber or Lyft to generate income. You can set your own schedule and drive as often as you wish. Of course, the more you drive the more money you'll make.

Boat Bound. Do you own a boat sitting in dry dock? Does your boat only see water on Memorial and Labor Day? If so, you can use Boat Bound to rent it out rather than have it resting on a trailer in your driveway.

RV Share. Did you buy an RV on the day you retired with visions of driving across the country? You may have made one or two trips, but now your RV is stored on the side of your house and it's being used as an extra storage room. Through RV Share you can rent it out to generate income. RV Share has an earnings calculator to give you an estimate of how much money you can make from renting your Class A RV, Fifth Wheel, or Pop Up Trailer.

Turo. Through Turo you can turn your car into a rental. Your car probably sits idle for most of the day so now you can let others drive it when you're not using it, and this will put a few extra dollars in your pocket.

Just Park. A parking spot is a coveted asset if you live in San Francisco, New York, or Boston. If you own a parking spot, you can now rent it out through Just Park. In addition to traditional parking spots, you can also rent your driveway.

Airbnb and HomeAway. Do you have a room to rent? Do you own a second home? If so, you can utilize Airbnb and HomeAway to rent out your room or the entire home.

Silvernest. Are you an empty nester? Do you want a companion? Silvernest lets you screen for roommates who are looking for a place to live and share expenses. In addition to earning income you'll make a friend. This service is best suited for individuals in retirement and whose children are no longer living with them.

Rent the Runway. Do you have a closet full of clothes you haven't worn in years? You can rent them out and make some money. You can also rent clothes, reducing the need to buy clothes you may only wear once or twice. Fewer clothes means a smaller closet and less space.

Etsy. Are you creative? If so, you can sell your items on Etsy.

TaskRabbit. Are you handy? Can you assemble IKEA Furniture? TaskRabbit lets you put your hands to work through assembly, installation, or yardwork.

UpWork. Can you design websites? Create spreadsheets? Write papers? Do taxes? UpWork is a freelancer's dream in the new economy because you can work from home and help others across the country.

DogVacay. Are you a dog lover? DogVacay lets you walk or board dogs for others. You can generate income while walking a few dogs around your block!

These companies, and many more like them, may help you produce more income during your retirement. To generate this income, it might be time to examine your resources and talents to see if you can put them to good use. Happy Sharing!

We keep moving forward, opening new doors, and doing new things, because we're curious and curiosity keeps leading us down new paths. ~ Walt Disney

February 7, 2018

Dow Jones = 24,893.35

128 My Friend Timms

Timms is one of the hardest working men I've ever met. I met him about 10 years ago while visiting his company to offer financial planning and investment management services to the executives. He's the security guard.

He knew I was meeting with the executives in the C-Suite but asked if I could meet with him in between my appointments. I told him I could, so we scheduled a quick meeting. When we met he informed me he had less than $1,000 to invest and he had to work two jobs to make ends meet. However, he just became eligible to enroll in the 401(k) plan and wanted some guidance. We discussed his options and selected five mutual funds based on his goals. We set up his plan to have an equal weighting to each fund.

In addition to selecting his investments we talked about the benefits of staying invested, investing monthly, and rebalancing annually. Over the past 10 years he's followed the script. He's also increased his annual contribution each time his company gave him a raise. The increases have been small but consistent.

I met with him recently and was surprised with his account balance. It's twice the average balance in the plan and it's rivalling those who make more money than he does. I was happy for Timms and his family.

Timms has become a good investor by adhering to time-tested investment rules like allocating his investments correctly and saving his money. He's a buy and hold investor who doesn't get emotional when his account fluctuates because he can't touch his money for another 10 to 15 years.

I look forward to my visits with Timms because of his enthusiasm for investing. He asks great questions and his knowledge of the market is increasing. We should follow his lead

Remember this: Whoever sows sparingly will also reap sparingly, and whoever sows generously will also reap generously. ~ 2 Corinthians 9:6

February 15, 2018

Dow Jones = 25,200.37

129 The Bionic Advisor

The Six Million Dollar Man was a television series during the mid-70s about an astronaut who was severely injured during a plane crash and was re-built to have super-human strength. His new bionic body parts included both legs, an arm, and an eye, making him part human, part machine. The opening monologue for the show was: "Gentlemen, we can rebuild him. We have the technology. We have the capability to make the world's first bionic man. Steve Austin will *be* that man. Better than he was before. Better... stronger... faster."

Robo-advisor programs are digital platforms with little to no human interaction.[1] They're attracting billions of dollars as investors look for low-cost, efficient investment options. Betterment, Wealthfront, and Personal Capital are a few of the popular programs and together they manage more than $22 billion. Individuals log in to a website, complete a questionnaire, and then a computer algorithm will build them a "personalized" portfolio. The robo-advisor then manages the account based on the client's profile.

These programs appear new, but they're not. In the early 90s, most brokerage firms like Morgan Stanley offered managed account solutions based on a client's goals and risk tolerance. After a client completed a questionnaire, a portfolio of mutual funds was invested for them and rebalanced because of

---

[1] https://www.investopedia.com/terms/r/roboadvisor-roboadviser.asp.

market moves. These programs were rules-driven, built on computer algorithms. They worked well, especially if a client committed to the program through rising and falling markets.

The difference between the old and new robo programs is the technology. The advancement in technology has allowed these programs to thrive.

What do you get when you combine a human advisor with a robo? A bionic advisor! A Certified Financial Planner coupled with a robust technology platform may be better, stronger, faster than a stand-alone robo. The human component will allow your advisor to meet with you in person and help verbalize your goals and direct you to the best investment solutions. In addition to investment selection, he can give you guidance with your company retirement plan, insurance needs, educational accounts, philanthropic activity, and much more.

Today, most independent advisors have access to dynamic trading platforms. Model driven, goal-oriented portfolios coupled with risk tolerance and rebalancing software allow advisors to create their own robo programs. Access to this robust technology allows your advisor to produce rules-based investment programs founded on your goals.

To work with a bionic advisor, consider the following items.

Make sure your advisor is a Certified Financial Planner practitioner who's a fee-only, fiduciary, registered investment advisor.

A View from the Perch

Complete a financial plan so your advisor can help you quantify your hopes, dreams and fears. You can link all your accounts (checking, saving, credit, investment, etc.) through aggregator websites to update your plan in real time.

Stress test your portfolio to see how it may perform in up or down markets. Risk tolerance software will also help your advisor design a portfolio for you based on your risk level and financial goals.

Invest in low cost mutual funds managed by Dimensional Fund Advisors or Vanguard. Controlling your cost will allow you to keep more of what you earn.

Review your plan and investments by talking to your advisor on a regular basis.

Successful investing requires a combination of all the tools and resources available to you, and rarely is it an either/or scenario. A bionic advisor can't run 60 miles-per-hour, but he can help you build a solid portfolio!

We are all now connected by the Internet, like neurons in a giant brain. ~ Stephen Hawking

March 26, 2018

Dow Jones = 24,202.60

130 New Beginnings

Thank you for joining me on my journey! I hope you found the stories timely and beneficial. As you write your own investment story, focus on your financial plan. It will help you quantify your financial goals and dreams. Your plan will remove confusion, complexity, and worry from the investment management process, allowing you to enjoy life.

As my book ends and your story begins, I'll leave you with a few key ideas highlighted throughout the pages to help make you a better investor.

- **Create a financial plan.** Investors who complete a financial plan have three times more assets than those individuals who did little or no planning.[1]
- **Stocks outperform bonds.** The 90-year average annual return for stocks has been 10% compared to 5.6% for long-term government bonds. A $1 investment 90 years ago in large company stocks is now worth $5,386 while $1 invested in bonds is worth $132.[2]
- **Small company stocks outperform large company stocks.** The Dimensional U.S. Small Cap Value Index averaged 13.3% from 1928 to 2015.

---

[1] http://www.nber.org/papers/w17078.pdf.
[2] Dimensional Funds 2016 Matrix Book.

A $1 investment grew to $58,263. The Dimensional Large Cap Value Index averaged 11.1%. A dollar investment in the large cap index grew to $10,414.[3]

- **Diversification is safer than concentration.** A portfolio of large, small, and international stocks will give you exposure to companies from around the globe. Adjusting your portfolio from 100% stocks to 60% stocks and 40% bonds will reduce your risk by 24%.[4]
- **Passive index investing is better than active stock picking.** The Standard & Poor's study of passive vs. active investing reveals that over a 15-year period 95% of active fund managers fail to outperform their benchmark. Passive investing also outperforms active over 1, 3, 5, and 10 years.[5]
- **The less you pay in fees the higher your return.** This is obvious but needs to be stated. Less is more.
- **Working with an investment advisor may increase your returns.** A study by Vanguard

---

[3] Ibid.
[4] Morningstar Office Hypothetical Tool.
[5] https://us.spindices.com/documents/spiva/spiva-us-year-end-2016.pdf.

revealed that an advisor relationship can add 3% in net returns.[6] An advisor can help you with multiple levels of planning including financial, estate, investment, charitable, and much more. If you're going to work with an advisor, make sure he's a Certified Financial Planner™ or Chartered Financial Analysis.

Two are better than one, because they have a good return for their labor: If either of them falls down, one can help the other up. ~ Ecclesiastes 4:9

---

[6] https://www.vanguard.com/pdf/ISGQVAA.pdf.

Notes and Disclaimers

Investments aren't guaranteed, and they do involve risk.

Your returns may differ from those listed in this book.

The information and data in this book is not a solicitation to buy or sell securities.

The data in each blog post including price, valuations, returns, yields, positions, and names are for the date of the blog post only, and the information may change based on new information.

"Today," "year-to-date," or "now" refer to the date the blog post was written, which can be found at the end of each chapter.

Options involve risk and aren't suitable for every investor. Please refer to Characteristics and Risks of Standardized Options for more information on trading options.

The returns and valuations do not include fees or taxes unless otherwise noted.

For tax or legal advice please refer to your CPA or attorney.

A View from the Perch

Bill Parrott is the founder and owner of Parrott Wealth Management, a financial planning and investment management firm. www.parrottwealth.com.

Bill earned his Bachelor of Business Administration from the University of San Diego in 1988. In 2003 he obtained the Certified Financial Planner designation.

He lives in Austin, Texas with his wife and daughter.

Photo Credit: Dawn Fry

Cover Design: Tim Schmidt

Made in the USA
Lexington, KY
10 December 2019